The Facts on File
CHILDREN'S ATLAS

David and Jill Wright

Facts On File
New York • Oxford

CONTENTS

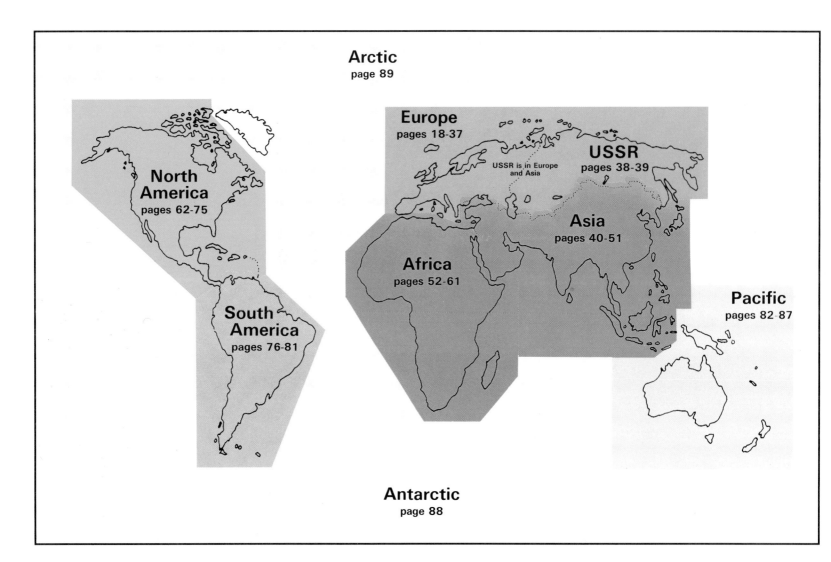

Arctic
page 89

North America
pages 62-75

South America
pages 76-81

Europe
pages 18-37

USSR
pages 38-39

USSR is in Europe and Asia

Asia
pages 40-51

Africa
pages 52-61

Pacific
pages 82-87

Antarctic
page 88

To Rachel and Steven

Text copyright © 1987, 1991 by David and Jill Wright
Maps copyright © 1987, 1991 by George Philip Limited

First published in the United States of America by Facts On File, Inc.,

First published in Great Britain by George Philip

Facts On File, Inc.,
460 Park Avenue South,
New York NY 10016

Library of Congress Cataloging-in-Publication Data
Wright, David, 1939–
    The fully updated Facts On File children's atlas / David and Jill Wright.
        p.   cm.
    Rev. ed. of: The Facts On File children's atlas / David Wright and Jill Wright. c1987.
    Includes index.
    Summary: Text, maps, and activities introduce regions and countries of the world.
    ISBN 0–8160–2703–X (acid-free paper)
    1. Atlases.   [1. Atlases.]   I. Wright, Jill, 1942–
II. Wright, David, 1939– Facts On File children's atlas.
III. Title: Facts On File children's atlas.
G1021.W686   1991 <G&M>
912—dc20

91–13725
CIP
MAP AC

Facts On File books are available at special discounts when purchased in bulk quantities for businesses, associations, institutions or sales promotions. Please call our Special Sales Department in New York at 212/683–2244 (dial 800/322–8755 except in NY, AK or HI).

Printed in Hong Kong

10 9 8 7 6 5 4 3 2 1

This book is printed on acid-free paper.

This atlas went to press in the fall of 1991, when the Soviet Union was undergoing considerable changes. The maps in the book reflect that nation's boundaries as of August 1991.

OUR PLANET EARTH

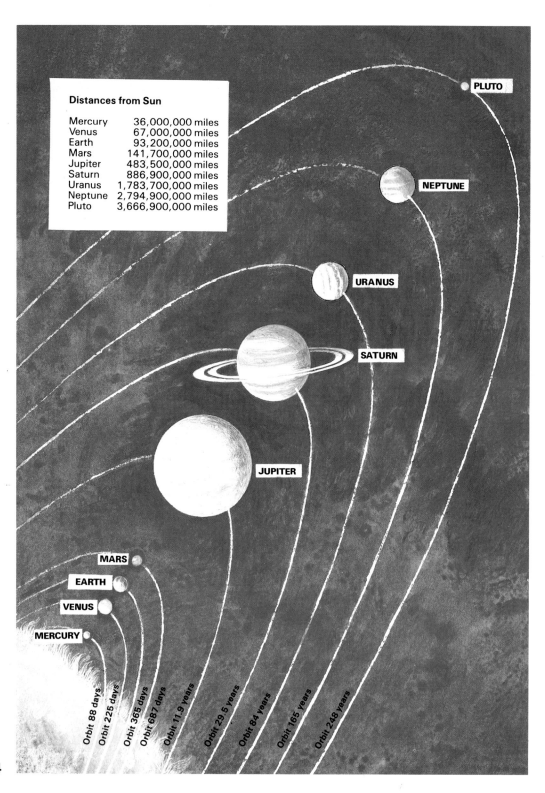

Distances from Sun

Mercury	36,000,000 miles
Venus	67,000,000 miles
Earth	93,200,000 miles
Mars	141,700,000 miles
Jupiter	483,500,000 miles
Saturn	886,900,000 miles
Uranus	1,783,700,000 miles
Neptune	2,794,900,000 miles
Pluto	3,666,900,000 miles

PLUTO

NEPTUNE

URANUS

SATURN

JUPITER

MARS

EARTH

VENUS

MERCURY

Orbit 88 days
Orbit 225 days
Orbit 365 days
Orbit 687 days
Orbit 11.9 years
Orbit 29.5 years
Orbit 84 years
Orbit 165 years
Orbit 248 years

Our planet Earth is one of nine planets that travel round the sun. The diagram (*left*) shows that we are 93 million miles away from the sun. It takes $365\frac{1}{4}$ days for the Earth to travel all the way round the sun – which we call a year. Every four years we add an extra day to February to use up the $\frac{1}{4}$ days. This is called a Leap Year. The Earth travels at a speed of more than 66,000 miles an hour. (In fact, you have traveled 370 miles through space while reading this far!)

As the Earth travels through space, it is also spinning round and round. It spins round once in 24 hours, which we call a day. Places on the Equator are spinning at 1030 miles an hour. Because of the way the Earth spins, we experience day and night, and different seasons during a year (see page 13). No part of our planet is too hot or too cold for life to survive.

Our nearest neighbor in space is the moon – 238,000 miles away. The first men to reach the moon took four days to travel there in 1969. On the way, they took photographs of the Earth, such as the one on the right. The Earth looks very blue from space because of all the seas. It is the only planet in the solar system with water. Look at the swirls of cloud, especially over southern Africa and over northern Europe. These show that the Earth has an atmosphere. Our atmosphere contains oxygen and water vapor and it keeps us and all other living things alive. We could not breathe on any other planet.

Fact box: Earth

Distance around the Equator
24,902 miles

Distance around the poles
24,860 miles

Distance to the center of the Earth 3958 miles

Surface area of the Earth
196,936,000 square miles (71% water; 29% land)

Distance from the Earth to the Sun 93,210,000 miles (It takes $8\frac{1}{2}$ minutes for the sun's light to reach the Earth.)

Distance from the Earth to the moon 238,906 miles

The Earth travels round the sun at 66,490 miles per hour, or 18.5 miles per second

The Earth's atmosphere is about 109 miles thick

The chief gases in the atmosphere are nitrogen (78%) and oxygen (21%)

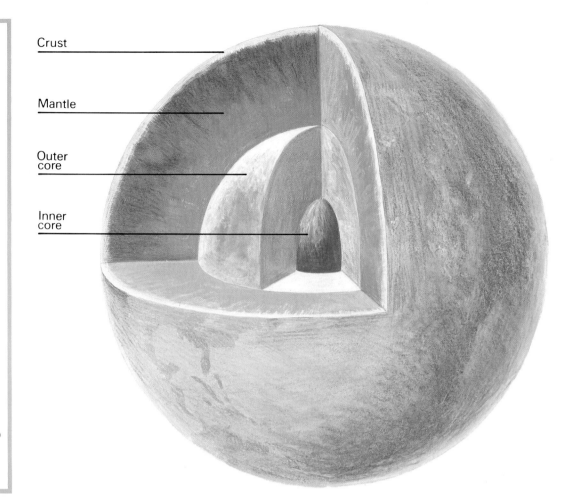

Crust

Mantle

Outer core

Inner core

Scientists believe that our Earth is made of layers of rock. The diagram above shows the Earth with a slice cut out. The hottest part is the core, at the center. Around the core is the mantle. The outer layer, the crust, is very thin under the oceans, but it is thicker under the continents. Scientists now know that the Earth's crust is cracked, like the shell of a hard-boiled egg that has been dropped. The cracks are called faults. The huge sections of crust divided by the faults are called plates and they are moving very, very slowly. Over millions and millions of years, the continents have gradually moved across the Earth's surface as the crustal plates have moved. Sudden movements near the faults cause earthquakes or volcanic eruptions. The satellite photo (*left*) shows all of Africa and a small part of South America. These two continents were once joined together, but about 100 million years ago they began to split apart.

MOUNTAINS, PLAINS AND SEAS

The map shows that there is much more water than land in the world. The Pacific is by far the biggest ocean; the map splits it in two.

Mountains are shown in relief on this map. Look for the world's highest mountain range – the Himalayas, in Asia. There are high mountains on the western side of both American continents. Most of the world's great mountain ranges have been made by folding in the Earth's crust.

Desert areas are in orange. The green expanse across northern Europe and northern Asia is the world's biggest plain.

Part of the Great Plains of North America. *The land is flat as far as the eye can see, but it is also 3280 feet above sea level. Plains are not always lowland.*

▽

Scale along the equator 1:116 000 000

0   1000km 2000km 3000km 4000km 5000km

1cm on the map = 1160 kilometres on the ground

0   1000 miles   2000 miles   3000 miles

1 inch on the map = 1860 miles on the ground

Fact box

Highest mountain Mount Everest, 29,028 feet (Asia)

Longest mountain range Andes, 4474 miles (S. America)

Longest rivers Nile, 4145 miles (Africa); Amazon, 4006 miles (S. America)

Longest gorge Grand Canyon, 217 miles (N. America)

Highest waterfall Angel Falls, 3212 feet (Venezuela, S. America)

Largest lake Caspian Sea, 139,266 square miles (USSR and Iran, Asia)

Deepest lake Lake Baikal, 6365 feet (USSR)

Largest ocean Pacific, 69,884,100 square miles

Deepest part of oceans Mariana Trench, 36,050 feet (Pacific)

Largest islands Australia, 2,967,900 square miles; Greenland, 839,766 square miles

Largest desert Sahara, 3,243,240 square miles (Africa)

West from Greenwich 0° East from Greenwich

COPYRIGHT. GEORGE PHILIP & SON. LTD.   180°

7

COUNTRIES OF THE WORLD

Five of the continents of the world are divided into countries. Most countries are now independent and manage their own affairs. A few of the smaller countries and islands are still ruled by another country.

Look at the boundaries between countries. Some follow natural features, such as rivers or mountain ranges. Straight boundaries were drawn for convenience. Often they separate people of the same language or tribe, and this can create problems.

The United Nations building, *in New York, USA. The world's problems are discussed here – and sometimes solved. Almost every country has a representative at the United Nations.*

B. = BHUTAN
BUR. = BURUNDI
BEL. = BELGIUM
L. = LEBANON
LUX. = LUXEMBOURG
N. = NETHERLANDS
R. = RWANDA
S. = SWITZERLAND
U.A.E. = UNITED ARAB EMIRATES

Scale along the equator 1:116 000 000

0   1000km   2000km   3000km   4000km   5000km

1cm on the map = 1160 kilometres on the ground

0   1000miles   2000miles   3000miles

1inch on the map = 1860miles on the ground

Fact box

Only five of the 'top ten' countries with large populations are also among the 'top ten' biggest countries. Check which they are. Asia has 6½* of the ten most populated countries – but only 2½* of the 'top ten' biggest countries.
*USSR is in both Asia and Europe.

Top ten countries by size (square miles)

1 USSR	8,649,489	6 Australia	2,967,900
2 Canada	3,851,788	7 India	1,269,338
3 China	3,705,405	8 Argentina	1,072,156
4 USA	3,615,102	9 Sudan	967,494
5 Brazil	3,286,470	10 Algeria	919,590

Top ten countries by population (UN figures)

1 China	1,134 million	6 Brazil	151 million
2 India	854 million	7 Japan	124 million
3 USSR	291 million	8 Nigeria	119 million
4 USA	252 million	9 Bangladesh	115 million
5 Indonesia	190 million	10 Pakistan	115 million

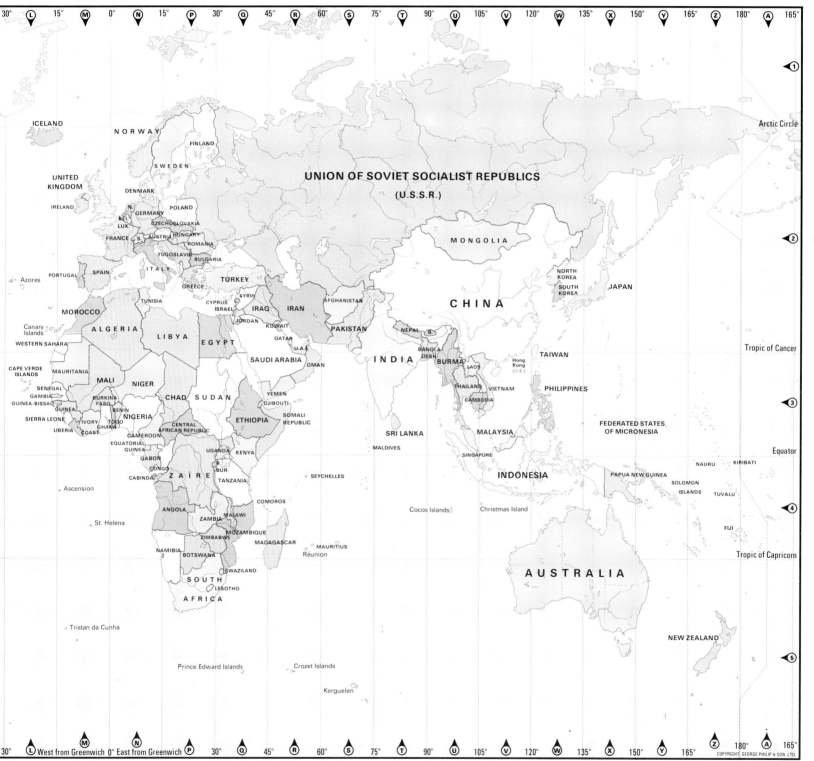

PEOPLE OF THE WORLD

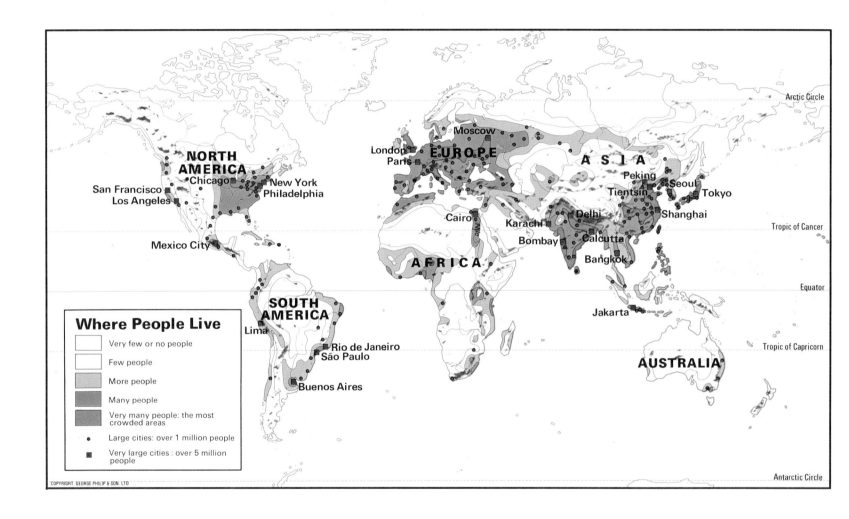

Where People Live

	Very few or no people
	Few people
	More people
	Many people
	Very many people: the most crowded areas
•	Large cities: over 1 million people
■	Very large cities : over 5 million people

There is *one* race of people: the human race. In Latin, we are all known as *Homo sapiens* – 'wise person.' The differences between people, such as dark or light skin, hair and eyes, are quite small.

But the differences in wealth are enormous. In any one country there are rich and poor people; but the differences between countries are even greater. The poorest countries are in the tropics – especially in Africa (south of the Sahara) and south Asia. People are about fifty times richer in some countries of the Middle East and northwest Europe, Japan, the USA and Canada. These are the world's richest countries.

Watering onions in the Gambia, West Africa. *This boy's watering can was given by the 'Freedom from Hunger Campaign', to help the family grow more food. Many schemes like this are helped by money from people in the* **10** *rich countries of the world.*

The main map (*opposite*) shows where the world's people live. Most of the world has very few people: notice that large areas are shown in yellow. Compare these areas with the maps on pages 6–7 and 14–15 and you will see that they are mostly desert, or high mountains, or densely forested, or very cold. So some remaining areas, where crops grow well, are very crowded indeed. Over half the world's people live in the lowlands of south and east Asia. Other crowded areas are parts of northwest Europe, the Nile valley and northeastern USA. The most crowded places are the big cities.

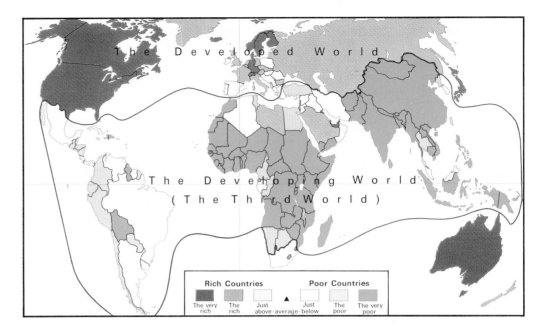

The Developed World

The Developing World
(The Third World)

Rich Countries			▲	Poor Countries		
The very rich	The rich	Just above-average		Just below-average	The poor	The very poor

Empty and poor: nomads in the Sahara. *Bedouin nomads drink a cup of tea in the Sahara Desert. They may be poor, but they are ready to welcome and help other travelers. The world's deserts are empty except where crops can be irrigated – as in the Nile valley.*

Crowded and rich: New York City. *The offices of Manhattan Island, in the center of New York, are crowded with workers during the day, but are empty at night. Only the richest people can afford to live in apartments here.*

▽

Crowded and poor: shanty-town in Brazil. *These shanties on a steep hillside in Rio de Janeiro were built by people who have nowhere else to live. Poverty in the countryside forces people into the cities, but it is hard to find a job if you have no skills.*

▽

The smaller map (*above*) shows the richer parts of the world where people usually get enough to eat, and the poorer parts where they are often hungry. Some of the poorest people live in shanty towns (see below).

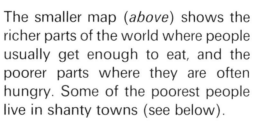

HOT AND COLD LANDS

Five important lines are drawn across these maps of the world: the Arctic and Antarctic Circles; the Tropics of Cancer and Capricorn; and the Equator. They divide the world roughly into the *polar*, *temperate* and *tropical* zones.

◁ **Arctic winter.** *Winter begins early in Greenland. These fishing boats are frozen in the harbor at Angmagssalik. From late September the days get shorter, until there are 24 hours of dark and cold at Christmas-time.*

The *polar* lands remain cold all through the year, even though the summer days are so long that the snow can melt.

The *tropical* lands are always hot, except where mountains or plateaus reach high above sea level. For some of the year the sun is directly overhead.

The *temperate* lands have four seasons: summer and winter, with spring and autumn in between. But these seasons come at different times of the year north and south of the Equator.

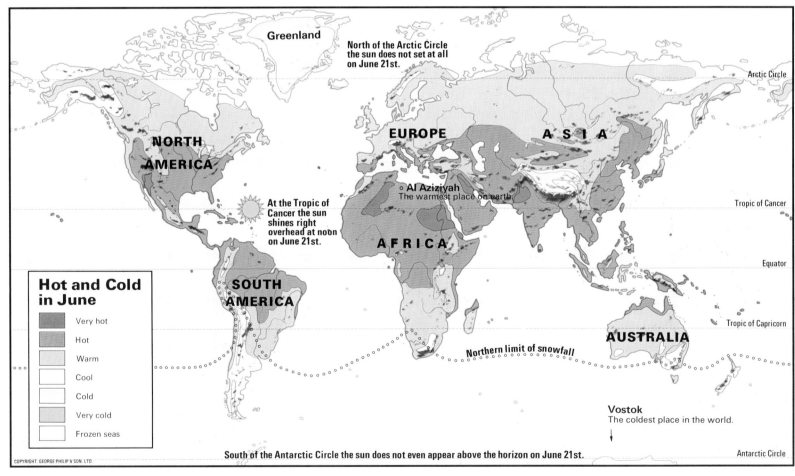

Greenland

North of the Arctic Circle the sun does not set at all on June 21st.

Arctic Circle

NORTH AMERICA

EUROPE

ASIA

At the Tropic of Cancer the sun shines right overhead at noon on June 21st.

○ Al Aziziyah
The warmest place on earth

Tropic of Cancer

AFRICA

Equator

SOUTH AMERICA

Tropic of Capricorn

AUSTRALIA

Northern limit of snowfall

Hot and Cold in June

- Very hot
- Hot
- Warm
- Cool
- Cold
- Very cold
- Frozen seas

Vostok
The coldest place in the world.
↓

South of the Antarctic Circle the sun does not even appear above the horizon on June 21st.

Antarctic Circle

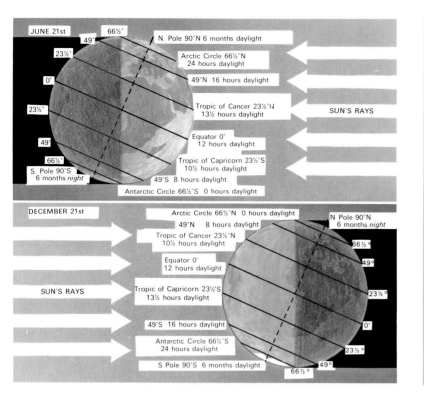

The diagrams above help to explain why the seasons vary north and south of the Equator. In June (*top*) the sun is overhead at the Tropic of Cancer. The North Pole is tilted toward the sun, and the Arctic enjoys 24 hours of daylight. It is summer in North America, Europe and Asia. Notice that Antarctica is in total darkness.

By December, the Earth has traveled half way around the sun. Spot the difference in December (*below*). Where is the sun overhead? Now Antarctica has 24 hours of daylight. It is summer in the southern continents, so children in Australia open Christmas presents during their summer vacations (see page 85).

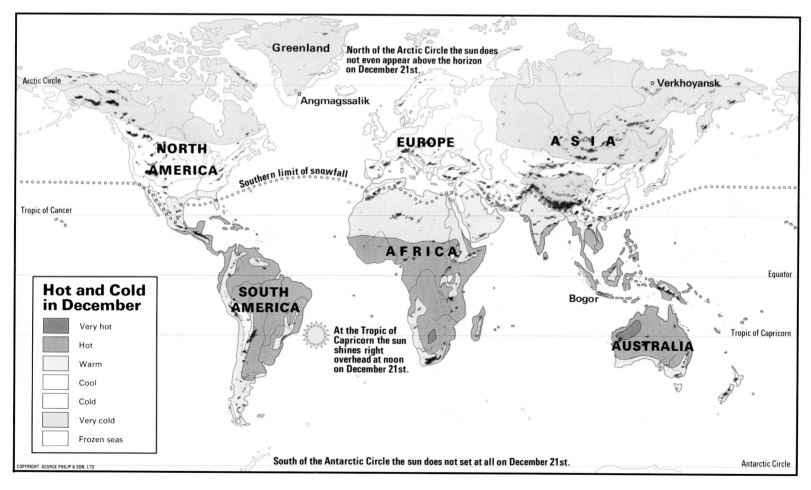

WET AND DRY LANDS

△ **Burning the savanna,** in northern Ghana, West Africa. At the end of the long dry season, farmers burn the bush (long grass and small trees). The land will be ready for planting crops as soon as the wet season begins.

Water is needed by all living things. The map below shows that different parts of the world receive different amounts of water. Follow the Equator: most places near the Equator are very wet as well as being very hot. The map opposite shows that near the Equator there are large areas of thick forest. Here, it rains almost every day. Now follow the Tropic of Cancer and the Tropic of Capricorn on both maps. The Tropics cross areas of desert, where it is dry all year. Between the desert and the forest is an area of tall grass and bushes called the savanna. People here talk about the 'wet' and 'dry' seasons. For part of the year it is as rainy as at the Equator; for the rest of the year it is as dry as the desert.

North of the Sahara Desert is the Mediterranean Sea. Places around this sea have lovely hot, dry summers, but they do have rain in winter. There are areas near other deserts with a similar climate, such as California in North America and central Chile in South America.

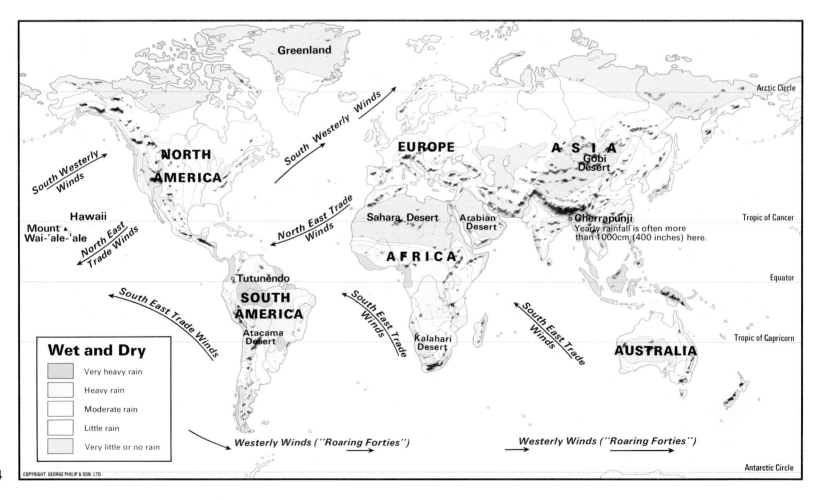

Forest and mountains in Alberta, Canada. The coniferous trees can survive Canada's bitterly cold winters. In the high mountains, trees cannot grow: it is too cold and the soil is too thin. Similar forests stretch across northern Europe and Asia, in Scandinavia and the USSR. The wood may be used for paper for books.

Desert in Namibia, southern Africa. The Namib Desert has given its name to the country of Namibia. It is a very dry area, west of the Kalahari Desert. Winds usually blow away from the land, so rain is very rare.

In the temperate lands, many places have some rain all through the year. Damp winds from the sea bring plenty of rain to the coastal areas, and trees grow well. London and New York have some rain every month. Far inland, near the center of the continents, and where high mountains cut off the sea winds, it is much drier. Here, there are vast grasslands, like the prairies of North America.

The Arctic and Antarctic lands are nearly as dry as the hot deserts. But the moisture collects as snow. Where the snow melts in the short summer, flowers and small plants grow in the marshy soil – called the tundra.

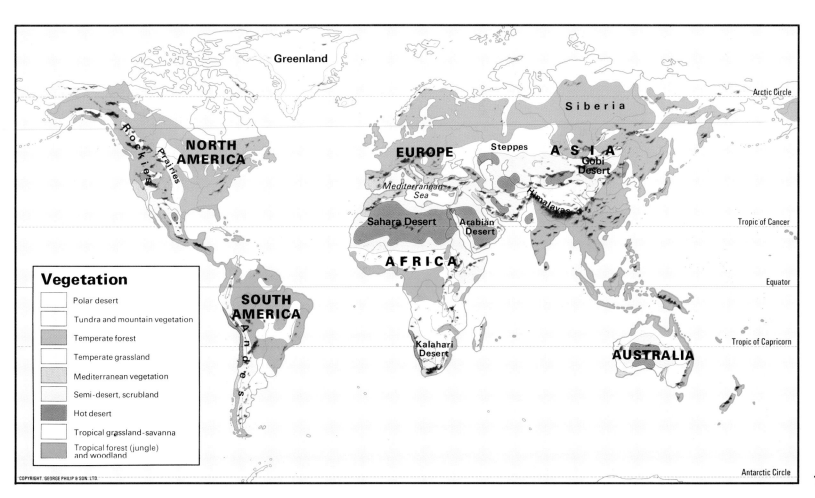

Vegetation

- Polar desert
- Tundra and mountain vegetation
- Temperate forest
- Temperate grassland
- Mediterranean vegetation
- Semi-desert, scrubland
- Hot desert
- Tropical grassland-savanna
- Tropical forest (jungle) and woodland

COPYRIGHT. GEORGE PHILIP & SON. LTD.

15

ENJOYING MAPS

An atlas is a book of maps. The maps in this book have been carefully drawn by cartographers (mapmakers) to tell us about the countries of the world.

The maps on pages 6 to 15 show the whole world. Because the world is round, the best model is a globe. It is impossible to draw a really accurate map of the round world on a flat piece of paper. This is why the Pacific Ocean is cut in half, and Antarctica becomes a long thin strip. On pages 88 and 89 there are maps of parts of the world viewed from a different angle.

The maps on pages 18 to 89 show the continents and countries of the world. Each map has a key, with information that will help you 'read' the map. Use your imagination to 'see' what the land is like in each part of the world that you visit through these pages. The photos and text will make your picture clearer.

These two pages explain the key to all the maps. The country of Ghana is used as an example. Ghana is in square

The border between Ghana and Burkina Faso.
The red lines on the map show the boundaries between countries. When traveling from one country to another, you have to stop at the border. These children live in Ghana, and the Ghana flag is flying on their side of the border.

The message on the arch says 'Bye-bye; safe journey'. In Ghana, most officials speak English, and people drive on the left. But in Burkina Faso officials speak French and people drive on the right.

B2 of the map (*right*). Find Ⓑ at the top of the map with one finger, and ➋ at the side of the map with another finger. Move each finger in the direction of the arrows; Ghana is where they meet. The stamps and photograph on this page come from Ghana.

The capital city of each country is underlined on the maps. The rulers of the country live in the capital city, and it is the biggest city in most countries. But not all capital cities are big. On this map, you can see three sizes of city. The biggest ones are marked by a square; they have over one million people. Middle-sized cities have a big dot, and smaller cities have a small dot. Small towns and villages are not shown on maps of this scale, but some have been included in this atlas because they are mentioned in the text.

Countries that are colored bright yellow on the map are shown in more detail on other pages. The small inset map shows where the main map fits into the continent of Africa. Maps of the whole of Africa are at the beginning of the Africa section (pages 52–53).

This is your chance to explore Africa – enjoy yourself!

Postage stamps

Postage stamps are on many pages of this atlas. You can learn so much from stamps! For example: the map shows you that Ghana is a country; the stamps tell you the official language of Ghana, and show you Ghana's flag.

The map tells you the name of Ghana's biggest lake (man-made). The 6Np stamp shows you the dam and tells you its name.

The map tells you that Ghana has a coastline; the 10Np stamp tells you the name of Ghana's main port, and shows you the big modern cranes there. Np stands for new pesewas (100 pesewas = 1 cedi).

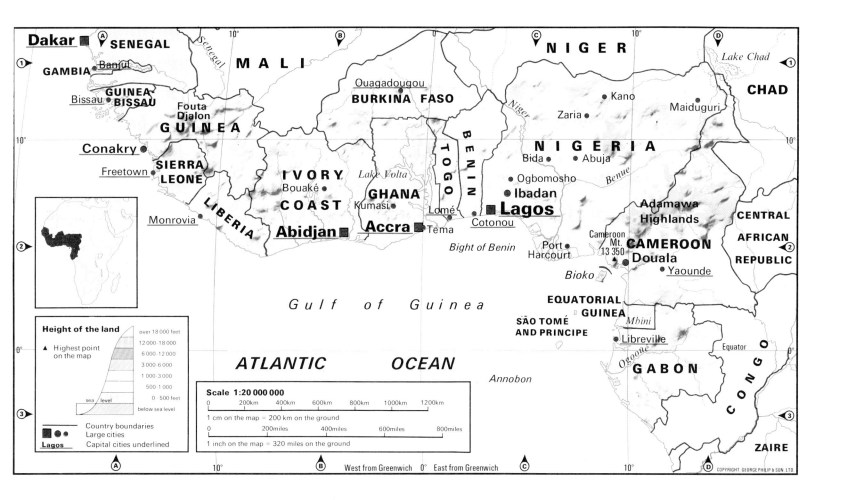

Scale

Scale 1:20 000 000						
0	200km	400km	600km	800km	1000km	1200km

1 cm on the map = 200 km on the ground

0	200miles	400miles	600miles	800miles

1 inch on the map = 320 miles on the ground

This box shows the scale of the map. The scale is written in different ways. The map is drawn to a scale of 1:20,000,000, which means that the distance between two places on the ground is exactly twenty million times bigger than it is on this page! Other maps in this atlas are drawn to different scales: little Belgium (page 24) is drawn at a scale of 1:2 million, while the largest country in the world is drawn at a scale of 1:45 million (USSR, page 38). Another way of writing the scale of this map is to say that 1 inch on the map is equal to 320 miles on the ground in West Africa. And this is how the scale line is drawn.

You can use the scale line to make your own scale ruler. Put the straight edge of a strip of paper against the scale line and mark the position of 200, 400, 600 miles, etc. (Or use the scale in kilometers if you prefer.) Carefully number each mark. Now move your scale ruler over the map to see how far it is between places. For example, Accra to Abidjan is 250 miles.

Height of the land

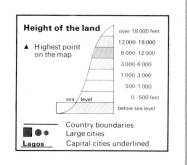

The countries of West Africa are colored so that you can tell the height of the land. Green shows the lowest land. Often the real land will not look green – in the dry season the grass is brown. The higher land is colored yellow or brown, even though some parts are covered with thick green forest! The highest point in West Africa is shown with a small black triangle – find it in square C2 – but the mountains are not high enough to be shown in mauve or white: look for these on page 44. And to find land *below* sea level, try page 24. Cameroon has some dramatic mountains (see page 57), but elsewhere the change from lowland to highland is often quite gentle.

Water features are shown in blue, and their names are in *italic print*. These include the sea, big rivers and lakes, such as *Lake Chad* (D1) and *Lake Volta* (B2). Blue dashes show rivers which dry up for some of the year.

EUROPE

The map shows the great North European plain that stretches from the Atlantic Ocean to the USSR. This plain has most of Europe's best farmland, and many of the biggest cities. To the north of the plain are the snowy mountains of Scandinavia. To the south are even higher mountains: the Pyrenees, the Alps and Carpathians, and the Caucasus Mountains of the USSR.

Southern Europe has hills and mountains by the Mediterranean Sea. The small areas of lowland are carefully farmed.

Puzzle picture
Western Europe's most important building.
★What building is it?
★Where is it?
★Why does it look so strange?
(Answers on page 96.)

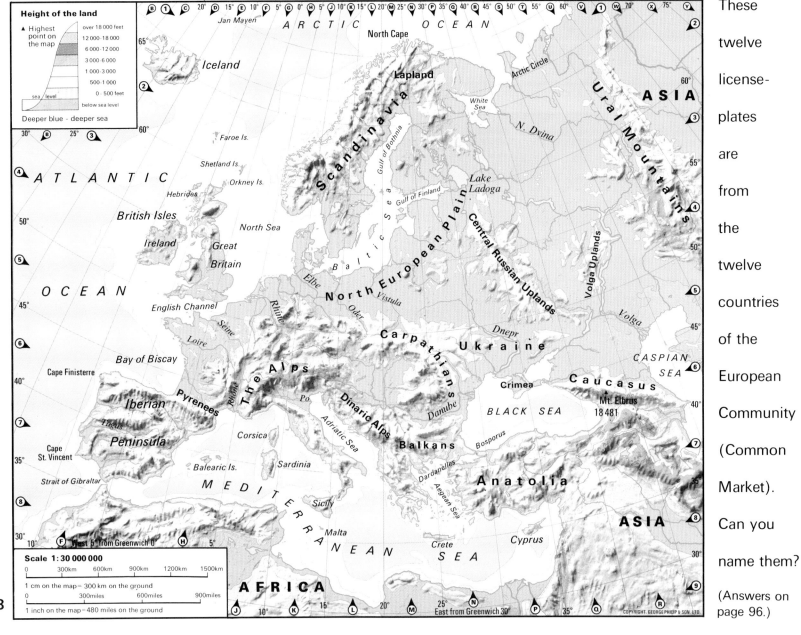

These twelve license-plates are from the twelve countries of the European Community (Common Market). Can you name them?

(Answers on page 96.)

Germany/Austria border. *There are many contrasts in Europe. This photograph shows farmland (foreground); woodland (centre); and mountains (the Alps, in the background); find the Alps on the map on page 18. Another important contrast is not visible. The foreground is in Germany, a big country; the background is in Austria, a small country.*

Fact box: Europe

Area 4,066,019 square miles (including European USSR)

Highest point Mt Elbrus (USSR), 18,481 feet

Lowest point Shores of Caspian Sea (USSR), 125 feet below sea level

Longest river Volga (USSR), 2293 miles

Largest lake Caspian Sea* (USSR), 139,266 square miles

Biggest country USSR*, 8,649,489 square miles (total area)

Smallest country Vatican City* (in Rome, Italy), less than one fifth of a square mile

Richest country Switzerland

Poorest country Albania

Most crowded country Malta

Least crowded country Iceland

*A *world record* as well as a European record

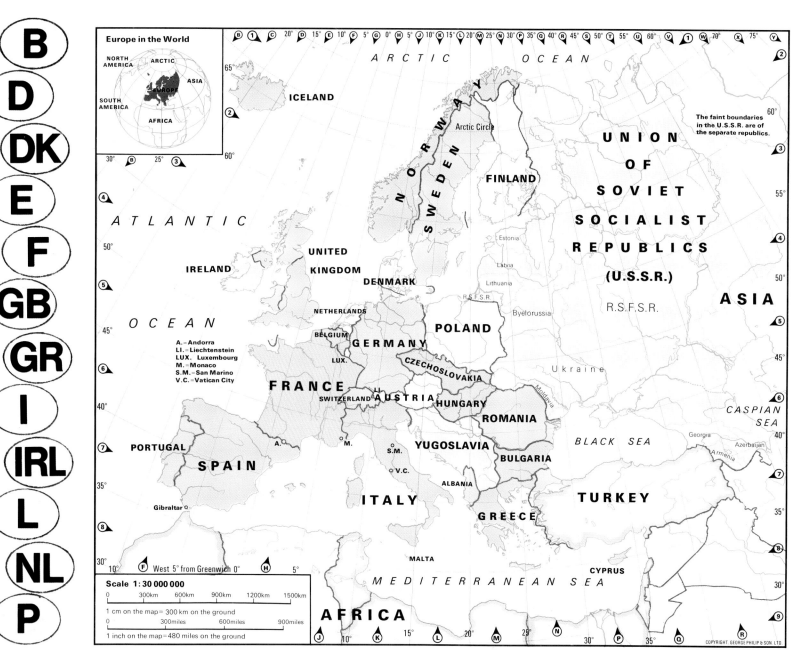

BRITISH ISLES

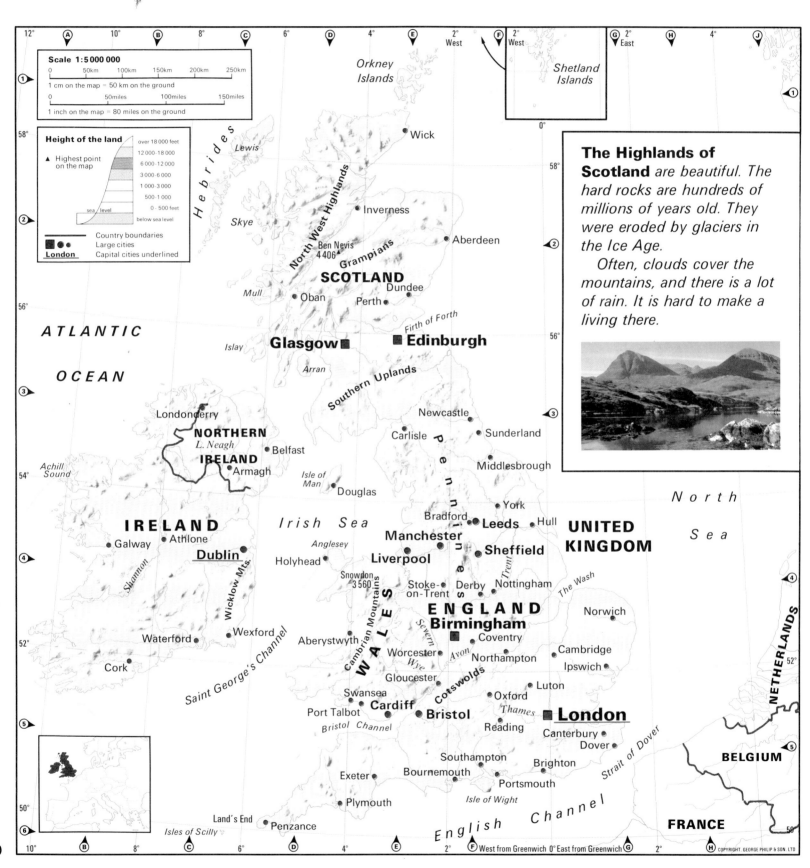

Scale 1:5 000 000

| 0 | 50km | 100km | 150km | 200km | 250km |

1 cm on the map = 50 km on the ground

| 0 | 50miles | 100miles | 150miles |

1 inch on the map = 80 miles on the ground

Height of the land

over 18 000 feet
12 000-18 000
6 000-12 000
3 000-6 000
1 000-3 000
500-1 000
0 - 500 feet
below sea level

▲ Highest point on the map

sea level

Country boundaries
■ ● ● Large cities
London Capital cities underlined

Orkney Islands

Shetland Islands

Wick

Hebrides

Lewis

Skye

North West Highlands

Inverness

Mull

Ben Nevis 4406 ▲

Grampians

SCOTLAND

Aberdeen

Oban

Dundee

Perth

Firth of Forth

Islay

Glasgow ■

■ **Edinburgh**

Arran

Southern Uplands

ATLANTIC

OCEAN

Newcastle

Carlisle

Sunderland

Londonderry

NORTHERN

L. Neagh

Belfast

IRELAND

Armagh

Pennines

Middlesbrough

Achill Sound

Isle of Man

Douglas

York

IRELAND

Irish Sea

Bradford

Leeds Hull

Galway Athlone

Anglesey

Manchester

UNITED

North Sea

Dublin

Holyhead

Liverpool

Sheffield

KINGDOM

Shannon

Wicklow Mts.

Snowdon 3 560

Stoke-on-Trent

Derby

Nottingham

The Wash

Waterford

Wexford

Aberystwyth

Cambrian Mountains

W A L E S

E N G L A N D

Norwich

Cork

Birmingham ■

Coventry

Cambridge

Worcester

Wye

Avon

Northampton

Ipswich

Gloucester

Cotswolds

Luton

Swansea

Cardiff

Oxford

Thames

■ **London**

Port Talbot

Bristol

Reading

Bristol Channel

Canterbury

Dover

Southampton

Brighton

Strait of Dover

BELGIUM

Exeter

Bournemouth

Portsmouth

Isle of Wight

Plymouth

NETHERLANDS

Saint George's Channel

Land's End

Penzance

Isles of Scilly

English Channel

FRANCE

West from Greenwich 0° East from Greenwich

COPYRIGHT. GEORGE PHILIP & SON. LTD

The Highlands of Scotland *are beautiful. The hard rocks are hundreds of millions of years old. They were eroded by glaciers in the Ice Age.*

Often, clouds cover the mountains, and there is a lot of rain. It is hard to make a living there.

What do the flags mean?

The Union Jack is made up of three flags: the red-on-white cross (+) of St George (England); the white-on-blue cross (×) of St Andrew (Scotland); and the red-on-white cross (×) of St Patrick (Ireland) – although most of Ireland is independent! St David (Wales) is not included, even though Wales is part of the United Kingdom.

The Republic of Ireland flag shows a white stripe (for peace) between orange (Protestants) and green (Roman Catholics).

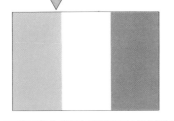

The Cotswolds, England, *are limestone hills. A little village built long ago from the limestone rock nestles at the foot of the hill, where a spring gives pure water. Woodland, grassland and ploughed land still cover much of England.*

The United Kingdom is made up of Great Britain (England, Scotland and Wales) and Northern Ireland. The UK was the most important country in the world 150 years ago. Many old factories and coal mines have now closed down, and several million people have no jobs. Unemployment is worst in the north. Much of the UK is still quiet and beautiful (see photograph above).

Can you spot eight famous London landmarks on this stamp? (Answer on page 96.)

Industry in South Wales. *This is the BP chemical works at Port Talbot, between Swansea and Cardiff. The big towers are cooling towers. The tall chimney on the right is part of the power station for the site. You can see sand-dunes in the foreground.*

The Republic of Ireland. is a completely separate country from the UK. There were twice as many people in Ireland 150 years ago as there are today. In the west, many abandoned

Ireland: harvesting reeds. *In the far west of Ireland, traditional scenes like this can still be seen in some places. But tractors are more common nowadays. This view is near Achill Sound.*

farms can be seen. Farming is still important, and Irish butter and cream are famous. New factories have been built in many towns.

SCANDINAVIA

Land of ice and fire

Iceland has many volcanoes. Most are quiet and peaceful.

But . . . sometimes a great volcanic eruption lights up the night sky and the light is reflected in the sea.

Only 250,000 people live in **Iceland**. It is near the Arctic Circle and there is ice on the mountains, in glaciers and ice sheets. The sea stays ice-free and is full of fish. Iceland has an important fishing fleet.

Sørfjord is a branch of Hardanger Fjord on the west coast of Norway. A fjord is a long, narrow, deep inlet of the sea with steep sides. Fjords were dug by valley glaciers in the Ice Age. Here the sides are so steep that the road is cut in solid rock. The cars show how steep and high the fjord sides are.

Forests and lakes in Finland.
Most of southern Finland is forested. The ice sheets scraped hollows in the rocks and there are lots of beautiful lakes. The trees are cut down for timber, wood pulp, paper, chipboard, matches and other products that are sold abroad.

The mountains of Norway and Iceland are high and rugged. There are ice sheets and glaciers even today. You can see snow on the highest land in the photograph of the fjord.

Southern Sweden and all of Denmark are lowland. This land was formed from sand and gravel brought by ice sheets in the Ice Age. The sandy parts do not have good soil, but the clay lands grow very good crops.

The five countries of Scandinavia have small populations. Most people live in towns and cities, and hardly anyone is poor. There are very few people in Lapland in the far north, which lies inside the Arctic Circle.

Reindeer in Lapland. *Lapland is the northern part of Norway, Sweden and Finland, where the Lapps live. They keep reindeer for their milk, meat and leather, and to pull sledges. Notice the warm and colorful clothes the Lapps wear.*

Gothenburg *is the main port on the west coast of Sweden. The sea does not freeze here for long.*

Legoland *is a model village beside the Lego factory in Denmark. Everything is made of Lego! This is a model of a fishing village in the Lofoten Islands of Norway.*

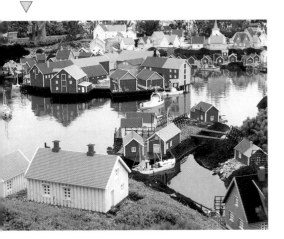

BENELUX

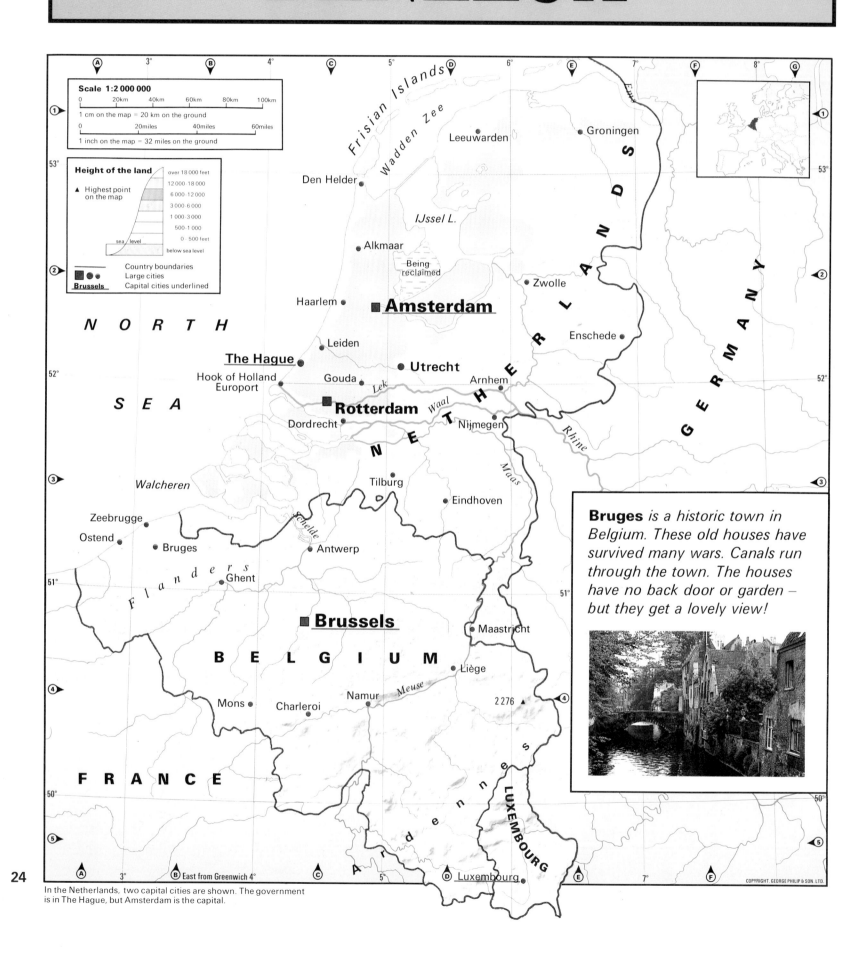

Scale 1:2 000 000

0   20km   40km   60km   80km   100km

1 cm on the map = 20 km on the ground

0   20miles   40miles   60miles

1 inch on the map = 32 miles on the ground

Height of the land

▲ Highest point on the map

over 18 000 feet
12 000-18 000
6 000-12 000
3 000-6 000
1 000-3 000
500-1 000
0 - 500 feet

sea level

below sea level

Country boundaries
Large cities
Capital cities underlined

Brussels

Frisian Islands

Wadden Zee

Leeuwarden

Groningen

Den Helder

IJssel L.

Alkmaar

Zwolle

N O R T H

Being reclaimed

Haarlem

■ **Amsterdam**

Enschede

Leiden

The Hague

Utrecht

Hook of Holland
Europort

Gouda

Arnhem

Lek

S E A

■ **Rotterdam**

Waal

Dordrecht

Nijmegen

Rhine

N E T H E R L A N D S

G E R M A N Y

Maas

Tilburg

Walcheren

Eindhoven

Zeebrugge

Schelde

Ostend

Bruges

Antwerp

F l a n d e r s

Ghent

■ **Brussels**

Maastricht

B E L G I U M

Liège

Mons

Namur

Meuse

Charleroi

2 276 ▲

A r d e n n e s

F R A N C E

LUXEMBOURG

East from Greenwich

Luxembourg

Bruges *is a historic town in Belgium. These old houses have survived many wars. Canals run through the town. The houses have no back door or garden – but they get a lovely view!*

COPYRIGHT. GEORGE PHILIP & SON. LTD.

24

In the Netherlands, two capital cities are shown. The government is in The Hague, but Amsterdam is the capital.

Spot the difference

What is the difference between these two coins from Belgium? And why is there a difference? (Answer on page 96.)

Europort, Rotterdam. *Rotterdam is by far the biggest port in the whole world: only a few of the docks can be seen here. Ships come from all over the world, and barges travel along the River Rhine and the canals of Europe to reach the port.*

Benelux is made up from *Bel*gium, *Ne*therlands and *Lux*embourg. Fortunately, the first two letters of each name are the same in most languages, so everyone can understand the word. These three countries agreed to co-operate soon after World War II. But they still have their own King (of Belgium), Queen (of the Netherlands) and Grand Duke (of Luxembourg).

The Benelux countries are all small and are the most crowded in mainland Europe, but there is plenty of countryside too. Most of the land is low and flat, so they are sometimes called the Low Countries. But Luxembourg and eastern Belgium have pleasant wooded hills called the Ardennes. There are lots of modern industries, but the coalfield of central Belgium is a problem area because most of the coal mines have closed.

Gouda market. *See the clogs for sale among the boots and wheelbarrows! Clogs are worn by some farmers and market gardeners, but many people prefer boots for working on the marshy land.*

Are these windmills?

No, these are *not* windmills! They are really wind *pumps*. They were used to pump water *up* from the fields into rivers and canals. The river is higher than the land! Much of the Netherlands was drained for farmland in this way. Nowadays, powerful diesel or electric pumps are used instead.

FRANCE

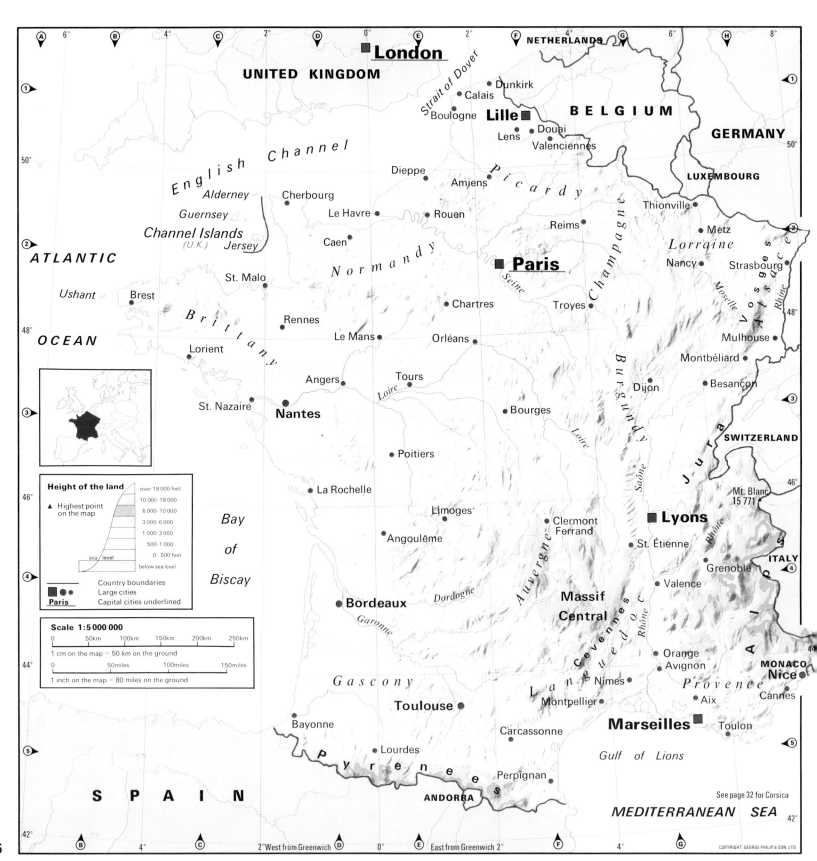

London

UNITED KINGDOM

Strait of Dover

Dunkirk
Calais
Boulogne
Lille
Lens
Douai
Valenciennes

NETHERLANDS

BELGIUM

GERMANY

LUXEMBOURG

English Channel

Alderney
Guernsey
Channel Islands
(U.K.) Jersey

Dieppe
Amiens

Picardy

Thionville

Metz

Cherbourg
Le Havre
Rouen
Caen

Reims

Lorraine

Nancy

Strasbourg

ATLANTIC

Normandy

Paris

Seine

Troyes

Champagne

Mulhouse

Montbéliard

Besançon

OCEAN

Ushant

Brest

St. Malo

Brittany

Rennes

Chartres

Orléans

Vosges

Moselle

Rhine

Le Mans

Burgundy

Dijon

Lorient

Angers

Tours

Loire

Bourges

Loire

Saône

Jura

SWITZERLAND

Nantes

St. Nazaire

Poitiers

Mt. Blanc
15 771

Height of the land

▲ Highest point
   on the map

over 18 000 feet
10 000 - 18 000
6 000 - 10 000
3 000 - 6 000
1 000 - 3 000
500 - 1 000
sea / level   0 - 500 feet
   below sea level

■ ● ● Large cities
Paris Capital cities underlined
Country boundaries

La Rochelle

Bay
of
Biscay

Limoges

Angoulême

Clermont
Ferrand

Lyons

St. Étienne

Rhône

Grenoble

ITALY

Valence

Scale 1:5 000 000

0   50km   100km   150km   200km   250km

1 cm on the map = 50 km on the ground

0   50miles   100miles   150miles

1 inch on the map = 80 miles on the ground

Bordeaux

Dordogne

Garonne

Massif
Central

Auvergne

Cévennes

Rhône

Gascony

Languedoc

Orange
Avignon
Nîmes

Provence

MONACO
Nice

Aix

Cannes

Toulouse

Bayonne

Carcassonne

Montpellier

Marseilles

Toulon

Lourdes

Pyrenees

Perpignan

Gulf of Lions

S P A I N

ANDORRA

See page 32 for Corsica

MEDITERRANEAN SEA

26

2° West from Greenwich   0°   East from Greenwich 2°

COPYRIGHT GEORGE PHILIP & SON LTD

French wine

A label from a bottle of French wine. The vines are growing in long straight rows on both sides of the valley. More wine is drunk in France than in any other country.

Market at Nice. *Which vegetables can you recognize on this stall? (Answer on page 96.) Every town in France has a good market. Housewives choose fresh fruit and vegetables very carefully.*

France is a country with three coastlines: can you see which these are? It is hot in summer in the south, but it is usually cool in the mountains and in the north. France is the biggest country in Western Europe, so there are big contrasts between north and south.

The highest mountains are the Alps in the southeast and the Pyrenees in the southwest. They are popular for ski-ing in winter and for summer vacations too. More than half the country is lowland, and farming is very important. Besides fruit, vegetables and wine, France is famous for its many different cheeses.

France is changing fast. The number of people living in villages is going down, and the population of the cities is growing – partly swelled by Arabs from North Africa who have come to live in France. The biggest city is Paris, which is also the capital. Ten million people now live in the Paris region, and five big new towns have been built around Paris.

Mont Blanc. *The 'White Mountain' is the highest mountain in Western Europe. It is 15,771 feet high. Even in summer (as here) it is covered in snow. Cable cars take tourists and skiers high up the mountain.*

Made in France

These *Majorette* models are made in France. They include a Renault van, a Michelin truck, an Air France bus and a Paris bus. The most popular French cars are:

Renault   Citroen   Peugeot

What else can you find that is made in France? In our home we have:

BIC ballpoint pens
a Le Creuset frying pan
ARCOROC glassware
ARCOPOL cups and saucers
a MOULINEX mixer
and a Philips washing machine

GERMANY AND AUSTRIA

The Rhine Gorge, in western Germany. Castles once guarded this important river route. The Rhine flows north from Switzerland, through Germany to the Netherlands. Big barges travel between the ports and factories by the river.

DENMARK

Baltic Sea

North Sea

Flensburg

Kiel

Rügen

Rostock

Lübeck

Frisian Islands

Schwerin

Hamburg

Oldenburg ● **Bremen**

Elbe

POLAND

Hanover

Bielefeld

Brunswick

■ **Berlin**

Potsdam

Münster

Magdeburg

Harz Mts

Göttingen

Essen ● Dortmund

Duisburg *Ruhr*

Düsseldorf

Kassel

Halle

GERMANY

Leipzig

Cologne

Erfurt

Gera

Dresden

Aachen ●

Bonn

Chemnitz

Rhine gorge

Ore Mts

BEL.

Koblenz

Neisse

Moselle

Wiesbaden

Frankfurt

Main

LUX.

Würzburg

CZECHOSLOVAKIA

Rhine

Mannheim

Heidelberg

Saarbrücken

Bohemian Forest

Nuremberg

B a v a r i a

Karlsruhe

Regensburg

FRANCE

Black Forest

Stuttgart

Danube

Freiburg

Augsburg

Danube

Munich ■

Linz

Vienna ■

L. Constance

Salzburg

Inn

LIECHTENSTEIN

Lofer

A U S T R I A

HUNGARY

SWITZERLAND

Innsbruck

▲ Grossglockner
12457

● Graz

Mur

I T A L Y

Klagenfurt

YUGOSLAVIA

Scale 1:5 000 000

| 0 | 50km | 100km | 150km | 200km | 250km |

1 cm on the map = 50 km on the ground

| 0 | 50miles | 100miles | 150miles |

1 inch on the map = 80 miles on the ground

Height of the land

▲ Highest point on the map

over 18 000 feet
10 000-18 000
6 000-10 000
3 000-6 000
1 000-3 000
500-1 000
0 - 500 feet
below sea level

sea level

■ Country boundaries
●● Large cities
Vienna Capital cities underlined

COPYRIGHT GEORGE PHILIP & SON LTD

East from Greenwich

Germany is shown with two capital cities. Berlin is the capital, but the seat of government is in Bonn.

Germany has more people than any other European country apart from the USSR. Most of the 80 million Germans live in towns and cities. Several million people called 'guest workers' have come from southern Europe and Turkey to work in Germany's factories. But nowadays there is unemployment in Germany, as in other European countries, and many 'guest workers' have returned home. Among the many different goods made in Germany there are excellent cars: BMW, Ford, Mercedes, Opel, Porsche, and Volkswagen.

There is also plenty of beautiful uncrowded countryside. The north is mostly lowland. Parts of the south, such as the Black Forest, are mountainous and popular for vacations.

Sausages, beer and pretzels *are popular in Germany. The beer from Munich is made from barley; the pretzels (dry biscuits) are made from wheat; the big sausages are made from pork.*

Germany was one country from 1870 to 1945. In 1990 it became one country again. From 1945 until 1990, it was divided into West Germany and East Germany, and there was a border fence between the two, with armed guards. To end World War II in 1945, Germany was invaded from west and east at the same time. The area occupied by the USSR forces became East Germany, with a communist government. The rest of Germany was called West Germany, even though it included southern Germany too!

Now, all Germany is one country again. But its area is still smaller than it was before 1945, because all the land east of the Rivers Oder and Neisse is now in Poland.

Berlin is the capital and the biggest city of Germany. From 1945 until 1990 it was divided into two. East Berlin was the capital of East Germany, but West Berlin was still part of West Germany – even though it was surrounded by East Germany. The Berlin wall divided the city; it was knocked down in 1989.

Transport stamps

Germany has excellent railways. The stamps show two clever answers to the problems of overcrowding: a double-deck passenger train, and a monorail above the River Wupper (near the Ruhr) to save space.

The Alps *are popular for winter sports. This guest house in the village of Lofer, Austria, is full of skiers in winter. Trees cover the lower slopes of the mountains: the skiers will go up to the snow slopes above the trees.*

Austria. Until 1918, Austria and Hungary were linked, and ruled a great Empire which included much of Central Europe. But now Austria is a small, peaceful country, which is friendly with both Eastern and Western Europe.

In the west of Austria are the high Alps, and many tourists come to enjoy the beautiful scenery and winter sports. Busy highways and electric railways cross the Austrian Alps to link Germany with Italy.

Most Austrians live in the lower, eastern part of the country. The capital is Vienna. It was once near the center of the Austrian Empire; now it is in a corner of the country.

The international clock *in Berlin, which tells the time of the whole world! It is 16.00 hours (4 pm) in Berlin: what time is it in Reykjavik (Iceland)? and in Helsinki (Finland)? And how does the clock work? (Answers on page 96.)*

SPAIN AND PORTUGAL

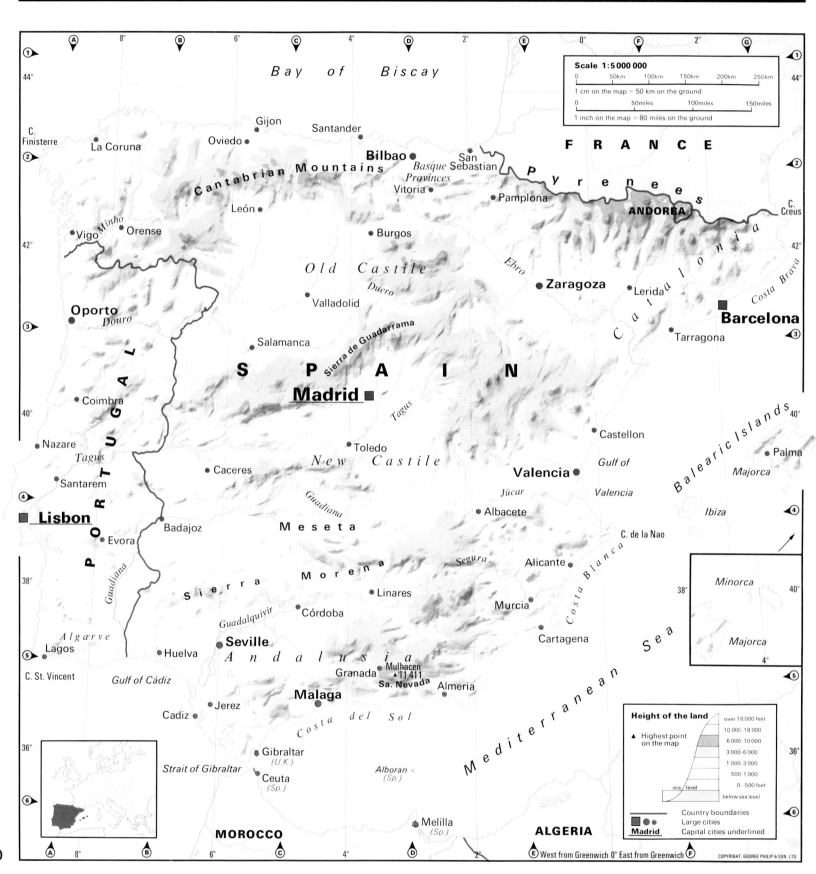

Bay of Biscay

Scale 1:5 000 000

| 0 | 50km | 100km | 150km | 200km | 250km |

1 cm on the map = 50 km on the ground

| 0 | 50miles | 100miles | 150miles |

1 inch on the map = 80 miles on the ground

FRANCE

Gijon
Santander
C. Finisterre
La Coruna
Oviedo
Bilbao
San Sebastian
Basque Provinces
Vitoria
Pamplona
Pyrenees
ANDORRA
C. Creus
León
Burgos
Vigo
Minho
Orense
Old Castile
Duero
Zaragoza
Lerida
Costa Brava
Ebro
Catalonia
Oporto
Douro
Valladolid
Barcelona
Salamanca
Tarragona
S P A I N
Sierra de Guadarrama
Coimbra
Madrid
Tagus
Castellon
Nazare
Tagus
New Castile
Toledo
Palma
Majorca
Balearic Islands
Santarem
Caceres
Valencia
Gulf of Valencia
Lisbon
PORTUGAL
Guadiana
Júcar
Ibiza
Badajoz
Meseta
Albacete
C. de la Nao
Evora
Guadiana
Sierra Morena
Segura
Alicante
Costa Blanca
Minorca
Algarve
Linares
Murcia
Majorca
Lagos
Córdoba
Guadalquivir
Cartagena
C. St. Vincent
Huelva
Andalusia
Mulhacen ▲11 411
Sa. Nevada
Almeria
Seville
Granada
Gulf of Cádiz
Malaga
Mediterranean Sea
Cadiz
Jerez
Costa del Sol
Gibraltar (U.K.)
Strait of Gibraltar
Ceuta (Sp.)
Alboran (Sp.)

Height of the land

	over 18 000 feet
▲ Highest point on the map	10 000-18 000
	6 000-10 000
	3 000-6 000
	1 000-3 000
	500-1 000
sea level	0 - 500 feet
	below sea level

Country boundaries
● ● Large cities
Madrid Capital cities underlined

Melilla (Sp.)

MOROCCO

ALGERIA

West from Greenwich 0° East from Greenwich

Village in southern Spain. *The old houses crowd closely together, and roads are very narrow: wide enough for a donkey, but not for trucks. People whitewash their houses to reflect the rays of the hot sun. Olive trees grow on the hills.*

Did you know?

Gibraltar is still a British colony, but it is only 2.3 square miles in area. Spain still owns two towns in Morocco: *Ceuta* and *Melilla*. Spain wants Gibraltar – and Morocco wants Ceuta and Melilla.

Spain and Portugal are separated from the rest of Europe by the high Pyrenees Mountains. Most people traveling by land from the north reach Spain along the Atlantic or Mediterranean coasts.

The Meseta is the high plateau of central Spain. Winters are very cold, and summers are very hot. Olives and grapes are the main crops. But cars are the biggest export from Spain nowadays. Both Spain and Portugal have fine historic cities, with great churches and cathedrals – built when they were the richest countries in the world.

Spain is very popular for holidays: the Costa Brava (Rugged Coast), the Costa del Sol (Coast of the Sun), and the islands off the coast are crowded in summer. In Portugal the Algarve coast is the most popular holiday area.

The Alhambra Palace, Granada. *This beautiful palace was built by the Moors (Arabs from North Africa). The Moors ruled southern Spain for hundreds of years, until 1492. The Arabs brought new crops and new ideas to Europe.*

Spanish coins

Spain became a monarchy again in 1975; the coin shows King Juan Carlos I.

In 1982, the World Cup was held in Spain; this special coin shows a soccer ball and the world.

Bullring and flats, Malaga. *The bullring is a big and important building in Spanish cities. High blocks of apartments are typical of modern Spain. In the background is the blue Mediterranean Sea. Malaga is a large port in southern Spain.*

Sun-dried fish, Portugal. *Sardines caught in the Atlantic Ocean are dried in the strong sunshine at Nazare, Portugal. Many of the older ladies wear black clothes, even in summer.*

SWITZERLAND AND ITALY

Labels from food exported from Italy: try making a collection yourself!

Sorano, *central Italy. Long ago the hill town was a safe place to live. The houses huddled closely round the castle and the church. Nowadays, a hill town needs a zigzag road to reach it.* ▷

Italy is shaped like a boot: its toe seems to be kicking Sicily! The shape is caused by the long range of fold mountains called the Apennines. The great Roman Empire was centered on Italy, and there are many Roman ruins. Yet Italy was only united as a country less than 150 years ago. Italy has lots of big factories. The Fiat car plant in Turin is one of the largest and most modern in the world.

△

Venice, *northeast Italy. Travel is by boat or on foot: there are no cars, because the 'roads' are canals.*

Swiss record breakers

Switzerland holds some amazing world records.

*The *longest* road tunnel is the St Gotthard tunnel (10.14 miles).
*The *longest* stairway is beside the Niesenbahn mountain railway, near Spiez. It has 11,674 steps!
*The *steepest* railway goes up Mount Pilatus. It has a gradient of 48%.

*And Switzerland has been at peace with everyone since 1815. That's quite a record!

Switzerland also has the *oddest* license-plates: CH is from the Latin name for Switzerland:

CH

Confederatio Helvetica.

In **Switzerland** most people live in cities north of the Alps. Switzerland is one of the world's richest countries, with modern banks, offices and factories.

Rivers, dams and waterfalls in the Alps are used for making hydroelectric power: trains, factories and homes in Switzerland all run on cheap electricity. Cable cars powered by electricity take skiers and tourists high into the beautiful mountains.

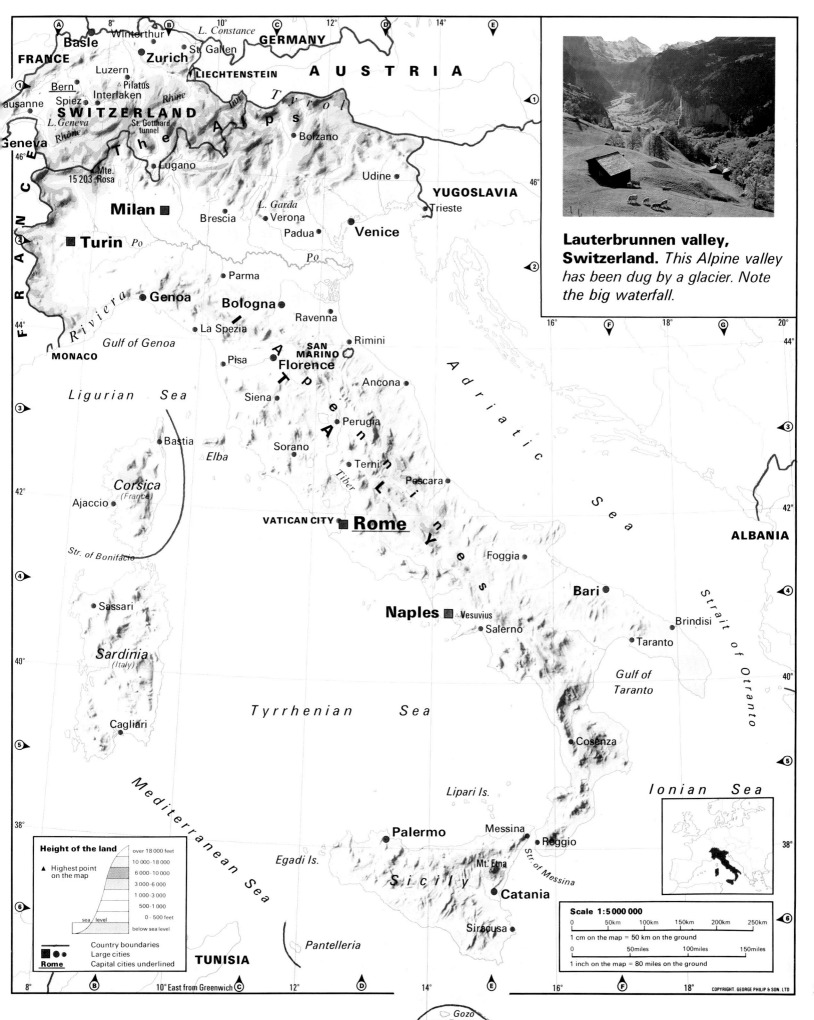

Lauterbrunnen valley, Switzerland. *This Alpine valley has been dug by a glacier. Note the big waterfall.*

A

8° B 10° L. Constance

FRANCE

Basle
Winterthur
GERMANY
Luzern
St Gallen
AUSTRIA
Zurich
LIECHTENSTEIN
Pilatus
Bern
Interlaken
Spiez
SWITZERLAND
Rhine
Tyrol
L. Geneva
St. Gotthard
tunnel
The
Alps
Rhone
Lugano
Bolzano
Mte.
15 203 Rosa
Udine
YUGOSLAVIA
Trieste
Milan
Brescia
L. Garda
Verona
Padua
Venice
Turin *Po*
Po
Parma
Genoa
Bologna
Ravenna
Riviera
Gulf of Genoa
La Spezia
Rimini
MONACO
Pisa
SAN MARINO
Florence
Ancona
Ligurian Sea
Siena
Bastia
Perugia
Elba
Sorano
Corsica *(France)*
Terni
Ajaccio
Pescara
Tiber
VATICAN CITY **Rome**
Str. of Bonifacio
ALBANIA
Sassari
Foggia
Bari
Naples *Vesuvius*
Sardinia *(Italy)*
Salerno
Brindisi
Taranto
Gulf of Taranto
Cagliari
Tyrrhenian Sea
Cosenza
Adriatic Sea
Strait of Otranto
Ionian Sea
Mediterranean Sea
Lipari Is.
Egadi Is.
Palermo
Messina
Reggio
Mt. Etna
Str. of Messina
Catania
Sicily
Siracusa
Pantelleria
TUNISIA

MALTA *Gozo*
Valletta

Height of the land

▲ Highest point
on the map

	over 18 000 feet
	10 000-18 000
	6 000-10 000
	3 000-6 000
	1 000-3 000
	500-1 000
sea level	0 - 500 feet
	below sea level

■ ● ● Country boundaries
Large cities
Rome Capital cities underlined

Scale 1:5 000 000

0   50km   100km   150km   200km   250km
1 cm on the map = 50 km on the ground

0   50miles   100miles   150miles
1 inch on the map = 80 miles on the ground

8° B 10° East from Greenwich C 12° D 14° E 16° F 18°

COPYRIGHT. GEORGE PHILIP & SON. LTD

33

SOUTHEAST EUROPE

Most of southeast Europe is very mountainous, except near the Danube River. Farmers keep sheep and goats in the mountains and grow grain, vines and sunflowers on the lower land.

The coastlines are popular with tourists. There are many holiday resorts beside the Adriatic Sea (Yugoslavia), the Aegean Sea (Greece and Turkey) and the Black Sea (Romania and Bulgaria). All these countries are trying to develop industry, but this is still one of the poorest parts of Europe.

Albania is the least-known country in all Europe: very few people are allowed to visit it. No railways crossed the frontier of Albania until 1985.

Yugoslavia is 1 country with 2 alphabets (Latin and Cyrillic), 3 religious groups (Roman Catholic, Orthodox and Moslem), 4 languages, 6 republics and 7 neighbors (can you name them from the map?). It is the biggest country in southeast Europe.

▲
Dubrovnik *is an old town on the coast of Yugoslavia. The walls are very big and impressive.*

▲
Romania. *Behind the maize (sweet corn) a huge modern factory brings jobs and money – and pollution too. The tractor and plough on the Romanian coin show that farming is still important. The Romanian language is not hard to understand. Try to read the words on the stamp.*

The Danube

The stamp shows a tourist boat at the gorge on the Danube River called the Iron Gates, on the border of Romania and Yugoslavia. The Danube flows eastward for 1056 miles from West Germany to the Black Sea. It passes seven countries, and is becoming important for trade. Dams and locks now allow big ships to navigate the river.

◁ **Fishing village, Crete.** *Crete is the biggest of the many islands that form part of* **Greece***. The village nestles below the mountains. Some of the fishermen's cottages have become guest houses for tourists.*

The Greek alphabet. *The Greeks developed their alphabet before the Romans, and they still use it. Some letters are the same as ours (A, B), and some look the same but have a different sound (P, H). The other letters are completely different. Some Greek letters appear in the Cyrillic alphabet, USSR (see page 39). The word* alphabet *is formed from the first two Greek letters:* alpha *and* beta.

A	B	Γ	Δ	E	Z	H	Θ	I	K	Λ	M	N	Ξ	O	Π	P	Σ	T	Y	Φ	X	Ψ	Ω
A	V/B	G	D	E	Z	E	TH	I	K	L	M	N	X	O	P	R	S	T	Y	F	CH	PS	O

35

EAST EUROPE

DENMARK

Baltic Sea

Gdansk Bay

R.S.F.S.R.

Lithuania

● Gdansk

● Elblag

● Olsztyn

● Szczecin

Vistula

● Bialystok

Bydgoszcz ●

● Torun

Warta

Bug

● Poznan

■ **Warsaw**

P O L A N D

● **Lodz**

Neisse

● Radom

● Lublin

G E R M A N Y

Wroclaw ●

Oder

Warta

● Kielce

Czestochowa ●

Vistula

Liberec ●

S i l e s i a

Ohre

● Bytom

Gliwice ● ● Katowice

Krakow

■ **Prague**

Labe

Krakow

C a r p a t h i a n

● Bielsko-Biala

B o h e m i a

C Z E C H O S L O V A K I A

Ostrava ●

Plzen ●

Olomouc ●

▲Tatra
8 711

● Kosice

M o u n t a i n s

Telc ● **Brno** ●

Morava

Bratislava

Miskolc ●

● Debrecen

Tisza

A U S T R I A

● Gyor

■ **Budapest**

H U N G A R Y

Danube

R O M A N I A

L. Balaton

Szeged ●

Tisza

Drava

● Pecs

Y U G O S L A V I A

Height of the land

▲ Highest point
on the map

over 18 000 feet
10 000-18 000
6 000-10 000
3 000-6 000
1 000-3 000
500-1 000
0 - 500 feet
below sea level

sea level

■ ● ● Country boundaries
Large cities
Warsaw Capital cities underlined

Scale 1:5 000 000

0   50km   100km   150km   200km   250km

1 cm on the map = 50 km on the ground

0   50miles   100miles   150miles

1 inch on the map = 80 miles on the ground

12° East from Greenwich

COPYRIGHT. GEORGE PHILIP & SON. LTD.

What can you buy from Poland?

In our home, we have: shoes from Poland; chairs from Poland; books from Poland; and jam from Poland. What can *you* find from Poland?

◀ **Ploughing the fields, Poland.**
Horses are still used for ploughing fields in many parts of Poland. Look carefully . . . . How many horses are pulling the plough?

Poland has a coastline on the Baltic Sea. There are huge shipbuilding factories at Gdansk. There are big factories in the towns in the south, too, where there is plenty of coal. Most of the country is flat farmland (see photograph).

Czechoslovakia has beautiful hills and mountains. The lower slopes are covered with pine trees. The Czechs live in the west of the country, and the Slovaks in the east. This country is the home of Skoda cars and Bata shoes.

Hungary is a small, flat country. Mostly it is farmland, but Hungary also has the biggest bus factory in the world. Buda and Pest were twin cities, on either side of the Danube River. Now they have become Budapest, the capital city (see photograph below).
Languages. Polish, Czech and Slovak are Slavic languages. Hungarian is a totally different language; it came from central Asia. You can see some Hungarian words on the stamps and on the boat in the photograph.

The seasons in Eastern Europe:

Winter can be very cold in eastern Europe, so cross-country skiing is popular. But summers are warm and sunny. Lake Balaton is a popular vacation area in Hungary.

Budapest, Hungary: *a vintage paddle steamer on the River Danube is passing the parliament building.*
▽

▲
Town square in Telc, Czechoslovakia. *The historic centers of towns are carefully preserved in Eastern Europe. Some have been totally rebuilt in the old style, after wartime bombing.*

USSR

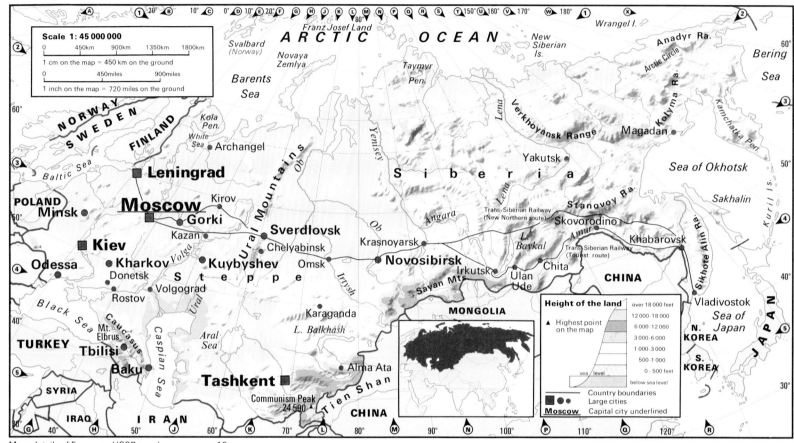

More details of European USSR are shown on page 19.

The USSR flag – the Red Flag

The hammer represents workers in industry, and the sickle represents farm workers. The red color represents the Communist Revolution.

USSR means
Union of
Soviet
Socialist
Republics

The USSR is by far the biggest country in the world: it is bigger than Canada and the USA together! In fact it is the biggest country in Europe *and* the biggest country in Asia as well. It is made up of 15 separate republics: the largest is Russia.

The Siberian steppes. *A lonely horse cart travels along a track in Siberia. The steppes are* not *steps! They are part of the world's biggest plain – snow-covered in winter, and with grass or wheat in summer.*

The USSR stretches across two continents, Europe and Asia. Most people live in the European part, west of the Ural Mountains. But gradually people are moving east to new towns.

Because the USSR is so huge, there are many different climates and almost all crops can be grown. The far north is snow-covered for most of the year (see page 89). Farther south is the largest forest in the world – a vast area of coniferous trees stretching from the Baltic Sea to the Sea of Okhotsk. Grassy plains, called steppes, extend south of the forest. In some parts, grain is grown on huge farms. The south is desert, hot in summer but cold in winter. With irrigation, crops like sugarcane and cotton grow well. And in the warm hills near the Caucasus Mountains, tea is an important crop. The USSR also has huge deposits of many different minerals and can supply most of the needs of its many different factories.

The Kremlin, Moscow. *There are three former churches in the Kremlin; it now houses the government of the USSR. The golden domes can be seen far away.*

The Cyrillic alphabet

Russian is written in the Cyrillic alphabet. This is partly based on Latin letters (the same as English letters) and partly on Greek letters (see page 35).

The alphabet was invented centuries ago by St Cyril, so that the Russian church could show it was separated from both the Roman and the Greek churches. In Cyrillic, R is written P, and S is written C. So the Metro is written METPO. CCCP (on stamps and coins) is Russian for SSSR (Soyuz Sovetskikh Sotsialisticheskikh Respublik), the initials of the country in Russian.

GUM shopping center, Moscow. *Local people go to GUM for shopping. The buildings are fine – but there are still long lines and shortages in USSR shops. GUM is short for Government Department Store in Russian.*

Trans-Siberian Railway

It takes over a week to cross the USSR by train and you must change your watch seven times. Here is the distance chart and timetable (only the main stops are shown).

Distance in miles	Town	Time (at Moscow)	Day
0	Moscow	2.30	1
595	Kirov	4.16	2
1130	Sverdlovsk	7.40	2
1688	Omsk	9.68	3
2077	Novosibirsk	7.55	3
2550	Krasnoyarsk	8.49	4
3221	Irkutsk	4.45	5
3509	Ulan Ude	1.07	5
3855	Chita	11.17	5
4544	Skovorodino	10.27	6
5301	Khabarovsk	10.35	7
5777	Vladivostok	1.15	8

*But local time at Vladivostok is 8.05 p.m.

Don't forget to allow another 8 days if you want to come back!

А	Б	В	Г	Д	Е	Ё	Ж	З	И	Й	К	Л	М	Н	О	П	Р	С	Т	У	Ф	Х	Ц	Ч	Ш	Щ	Ъ	Э	Ю	Я
A	B	V	G	D	E	YO	ZH	Z	I	Y	K	L	M	N	O	P	R	S	T	U	F	KH	TS	CH	SH	SHCH	–	E	YU	YA

ASIA

Asia is the world's biggest continent, stretching from the cold Arctic Ocean in the north to the warm Indian Ocean in the tropical south. Mainland Asia nearly reaches the Equator in Malaysia. Several Asian islands are *on* the Equator: Sumatra, Borneo and Sulawesi. In the west, Asia reaches Europe and the Mediterranean Sea, and in the east Asia reaches the Pacific Ocean, and gets close to Australia. In the center are the high, empty plateaus of Tibet and Mongolia.

◁**Himalayan Mountains, Nepal,** *photographed by the famous mountaineer Chris Bonington. The world's ten highest mountains are all in the Himalayas. Glaciers have carved the deep valleys.*

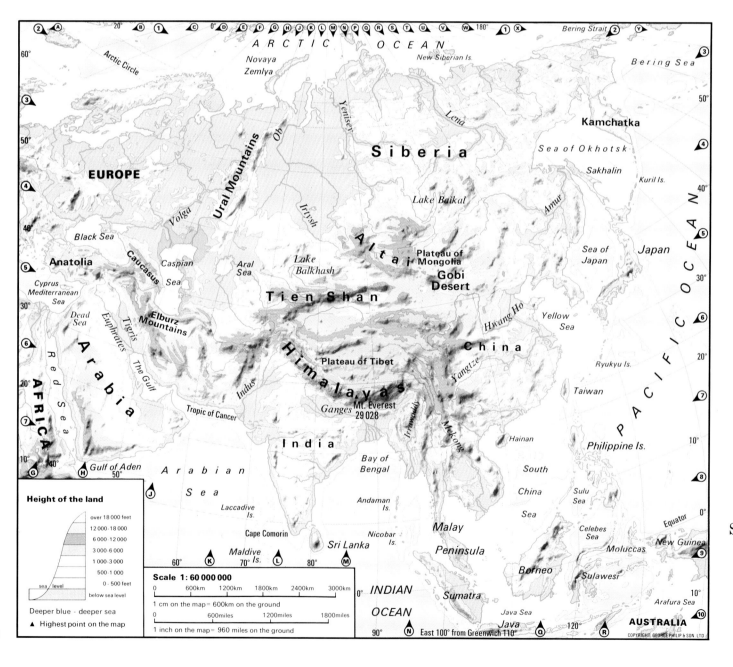

Height of the land

| |
| over 18 000 feet |
| 12 000-18 000 |
| 6 000-12 000 |
| 3 000-6 000 |
| 1 000-3 000 |
| 500-1 000 |
| 0 - 500 feet |
| below sea level |

sea level

Deeper blue - deeper sea

▲ Highest point on the map

Scale 1 : 60 000 000

0   600km   1200km   1800km   2400km   3000km

1 cm on the map = 600km on the ground

0   600miles   1200miles   1800miles

1 inch on the map = 960 miles on the ground

East 100° from Greenwich

COPYRIGHT. GEORGE PHILIP & SON. LTD

Money in Asia

Afghanistan
Bangladesh
Bhutan
Burma
Cambodia
China
Cyprus
Indonesia
Iran
Israel
Japan
Korea, N
and S
Laos
Lebanon
Syria
Macao
Maldives
Mongolia
Oman
Philippines
Qatar
Saudi Arabia
Sri Lanka
Thailand
Turkey
UAE
Vietnam

Fact box: Asia

Area 17,137,820 square miles (including Asiatic USSR)

Highest point Mount Everest* (Nepal/China), 29,028 feet

Lowest point Shores of Dead Sea* (Israel/Jordan), 1312 feet below sea level

Longest river Yenisey (USSR), 3442 miles; Yangtze (China), 3437 miles

Biggest country USSR* 8,649,489 square miles

Smallest country The Maldives, 115 square miles

*A *world record* as well as an Asian record

Buddhist shrine. *Religion is very important to most people in Asia. This Buddhist shrine is like many found in Nepal. It has been decorated with prayer flags and painted eyes.* ▷

Two countries cover over half of Asia: the USSR and China. India looks quite small – yet it is over ten times as big as Italy or the UK! But some of Asia's important countries are very small indeed, for example Lebanon and Israel in southwest Asia (Middle East); Singapore and Brunei in Southeast Asia (Far East).

Over half the world's population lives in Asia. The coastal areas of south and east Asia are the most crowded parts. Seven of the 'top ten' most populated countries in the world are in Asia: China, India, USSR, Indonesia, Japan, Bangladesh and Pakistan.

Some countries

Afghani
Taka
Ngultrum
Kyat
Riel
Yuan
Pound
Rupiah
Rial
Shekel
Yen

Won
Kip

Pound
Pataca
Rufiyaa
Tugrik
Omani
Peso
Riyal

Rupee
Baht
Lira
Dirham
Dong

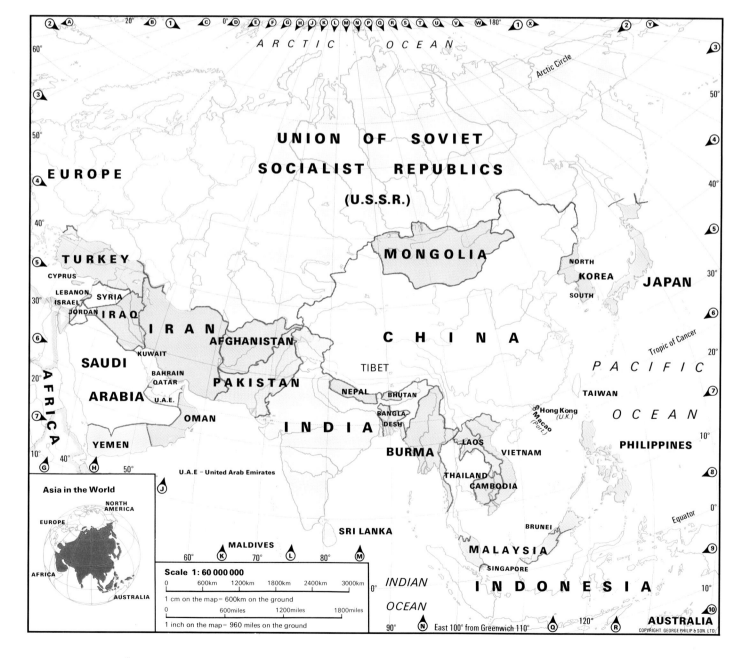

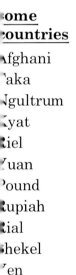

Asia in the World

U.A.E = United Arab Emirates

Scale 1 : 60 000 000

1 cm on the map = 600km on the ground

1 inch on the map = 960 miles on the ground

East 100° from Greenwich

COPYRIGHT. GEORGE PHILIP & SON. LTD.

MIDDLE EAST

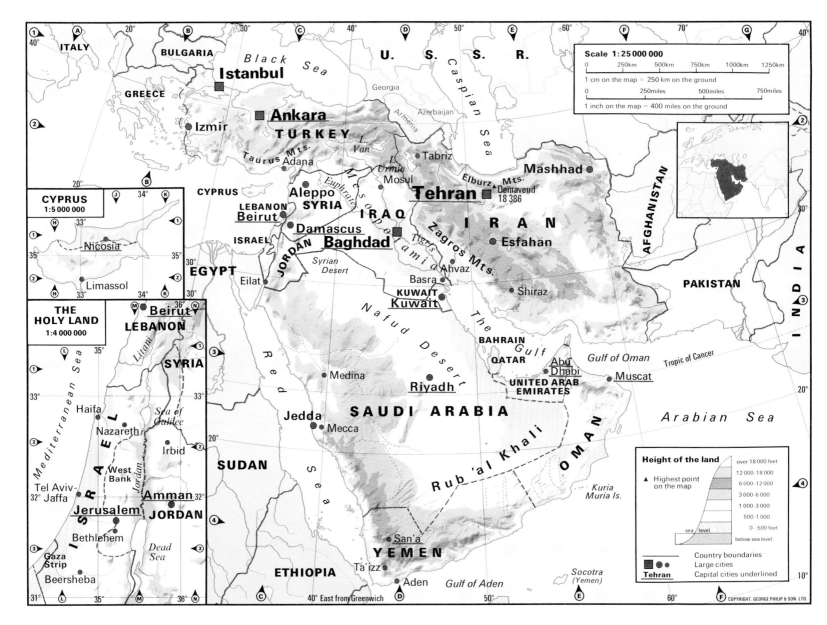

Map labels

ITALY
BULGARIA
GREECE
Black Sea
Istanbul
Ankara
Izmir
TURKEY
Taurus Mts.
Adana
U. S. S. R.
Georgia
Armenia
Azerbaijan
Caspian Sea
L. Van
L. Urmia
Tabriz
Mosul
Mashhad
Elburz Mts.
Demavend 18 386
Tehran
AFGHANISTAN

CYPRUS 1:5 000 000
Nicosia
Limassol

CYPRUS
LEBANON
Aleppo
SYRIA
Beirut
Damascus
Baghdad
ISRAEL
JORDAN
IRAQ
Euphrates
Mesopotamia
Tigris
Zagros Mts.
IRAN
Esfahan
Ahvaz
Basra
Shiraz
PAKISTAN
INDIA

THE HOLY LAND 1:4 000 000
Beirut
LEBANON
Litani
SYRIA
Mediterranean Sea
Haifa
Nazareth
Sea of Galilee
Irbid
West Bank
Jordan
Tel Aviv-Jaffa
Amman
JORDAN
Jerusalem
Bethlehem
Gaza Strip
Dead Sea
Beersheba
ISRAEL

EGYPT
Eilat
Syrian Desert
KUWAIT
Kuwait
Nafud Desert
BAHRAIN
QATAR
Gulf
Abu Dhabi
UNITED ARAB EMIRATES
Gulf of Oman
Muscat
Tropic of Cancer
Red Sea
Medina
Riyadh
SAUDI ARABIA
Jedda
Mecca
The Gulf
Rub 'al Khali
OMAN
Arabian Sea
SUDAN
San'a
YEMEN
Ta'izz
ETHIOPIA
Aden
Gulf of Aden
Socotra (Yemen)
Kuria Muria Is.

Scale 1:25 000 000
0 250km 500km 750km 1000km 1250km
1 cm on the map = 250 km on the ground
0 250miles 500miles 750miles
1 inch on the map = 400 miles on the ground

Height of the land
▲ Highest point on the map	over 18 000 feet
	12 000-18 000
	6 000-12 000
	3 000-6 000
	1 000-3 000
	500-1 000
	0 - 500 feet
sea level	below sea level

─── Country boundaries
■ ●● Large cities
Tehran — Capital cities underlined

40° East from Greenwich
COPYRIGHT. GEORGE PHILIP & SON. LTD.

▷ Holy cities of the Middle East.

In Jerusalem (*left*), Jews worship at the Wailing Wall, all that remains of the Jewish temple. *Jerusalem* is a holy city for people of three religions: Judaism, Christianity and Islam. People of all three religions live here and pilgrims and tourists visit the city.

Mecca (*right*) is the holiest city of ▷ Islam: it is where the prophet Moham-med was born. Moslems come from many countries to worship here.

Lands of the books

Three great religions started in the Middle East: Judaism, Christianity and Islam.

The Jewish scriptures are written in Hebrew. This is the world's oldest written language still in use today and reads from right to left across the page.

The Christian Bible consists of the Jewish scriptures (the Old Testament), plus the New Testament, which was originally written in Greek.

The Koran is the holy book of Islam. It is written in Arabic, which is also read from right to left.

The Jewish scriptures are written in Hebrew. ▽

The Koran is written in Arabic. ▽

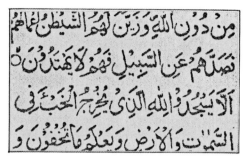

△

Oil in the Middle East. *The photograph above, taken in Iran, shows camels in the desert . . . a view that has not changed for centuries. But the flares and smoke in the distance are a clue to the biggest change in the Middle East: oil. Oil is pumped out from deep underground, and piped to ports for export to many countries in Europe, Asia and Africa. It is used for diesel, petroleum, paraffin and chemicals.*

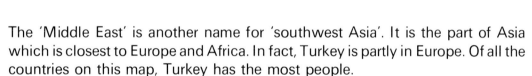

The 'Middle East' is another name for 'southwest Asia'. It is the part of Asia which is closest to Europe and Africa. In fact, Turkey is partly in Europe. Of all the countries on this map, Turkey has the most people.

Most of the Middle East is semi-desert or desert. Yet many great civilizations have existed here, such as the Assyrian, the Babylonian and the Persian. Their monuments are found in the fertile valleys of the largest rivers, the Tigris and the Euphrates.

Scarce water is used to irrigate crops in some places. In others, herds of sheep and goats are kept. Dates from Iraq come from desert oases; oranges come from irrigated land in Israel.

△

Progress in Qatar. *The big bulldozer was imported from England, to help build the new road. In the background you can see new skyscrapers and a big crane. Oil has made some countries in the Middle East very rich, especially those near The Gulf, like Saudi Arabia, Kuwait and Qatar.*

◁ **Winnowing wheat in Turkey.**
The gentle evening breeze separates the grain from the chaff: the heavier grain falls down, while the lighter chaff blows away. Winnowing is hard work! It has been done by hand for thousands of years: the old methods are still commonly used in many parts of the Middle East.

SOUTH ASIA

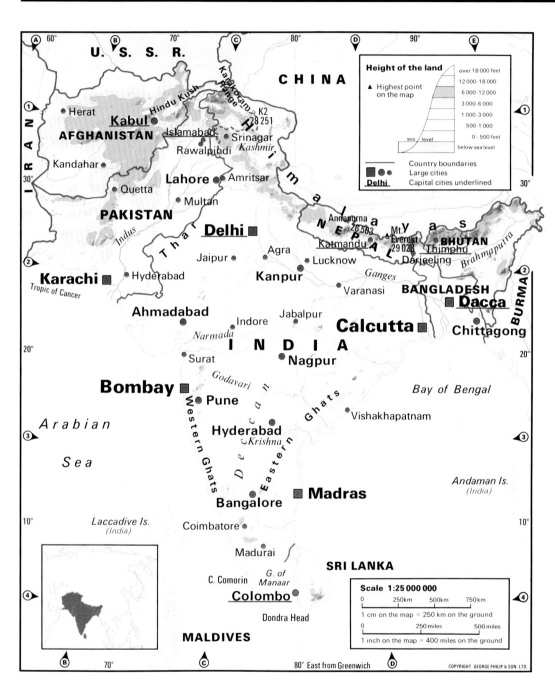

The world's highest mountains appear on this map, including Mount Everest. The Himalayas form a great mountain chain which joins on to other high mountain areas, such as the Hindu Kush.

Afghanistan is a rugged and mountainous country. Five other countries share the peninsula which stretches southwards from the Himalayas. **Bhutan** and **Nepal** are small mountain kingdoms.

Bangladesh is quite different: it is mostly flat, low-lying land where the great rivers Ganges and Brahmaputra reach the sea. In the west, **Pakistan** is a desert country, but the Indus River is used to irrigate crops.

India is the largest country. It stretches 2050 miles from Kashmir to Cape Comorin. Until 1947, Pakistan and Bangladesh were part of the Indian Empire, ruled by Britain.

Sri Lanka is an island country off the south coast of India. Farther south, in the Indian Ocean, a chain of islands makes up the country called **The Maldives.**

More than a billion people live in south Asia. The deserts and mountains do not have many people, but the river valleys, plains and plateaus are crowded.

Sri Lanka *means Resplendent Isle. This country used to be called Ceylon.*

Tea is an important crop in the hills where there is plenty of rain. Women pick the young leaves from the bushes (right), then they are dried and crushed and packed into tea-chests. Ceylon tea (left) is one of Sri Lanka's most important exports. Where does the tea you drink come from?

△
Planting rice, Bangladesh. *These men are planting rice seedlings in the wet soil. Sometimes monsoon floods can wash away the seedlings.*

Rice is an important food crop in south Asia. It grows best where the land is flat, and where the weather is hot and wet. The seeds are planted in a 'nursery' bed just before the monsoon rains are due (see below). When the fields are flooded, the seedlings are planted in the mud. In a good year, rice grows in the wet fields and is ready for harvesting after four or five months. If the monsoon fails and there is a drought, the seedlings will shrivel up. If the rice crop fails, many people go hungry. In areas where irrigation is available, the farmer can control the water supply and may be able to grow two rice crops a year.

Religion is very important in the lives of people in south Asia. Hinduism is the oldest religion, and most people in India and Nepal are Hindus. Buddhism began in India, but only Sri Lanka and Bhutan are mainly Buddhist today. Afghanistan, Pakistan and Bangladesh are Islamic countries. Many Sikhs live in northern India; there are also Christian groups in all these countries.

India's flag *shows that people of different religions are united in one country. The orange stripe is for Hindus; the green for Moslems; and the white for peace, with the wheel of Ashoka for Buddhists.*

Wool for carpets. *This lady in northern India is winding wool which will be used to make carpets. She sits in the courtyard of her house, where the ploughs and pots and pans are also kept.*
▽

The monsoon

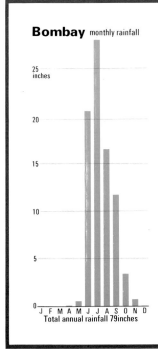

Bombay monthly rainfall

25 inches
20
15
10
5
0
J F M A M J J A S O N D
Total annual rainfall 79 inches

Most rain falls in one season, called the monsoon. In Bombay the monsoon begins in June (*left*) and the rain pours down for a few weeks (*right*). There are heavy showers in August and September, and then hardly any more rain until next June. From October to March the weather is cool and dry, then it gets hotter and hotter until the monsoon rains begin.

Northeast India and Bangladesh have even more rain than Bombay. But large areas of northwest India are desert.

SOUTHEAST ASIA

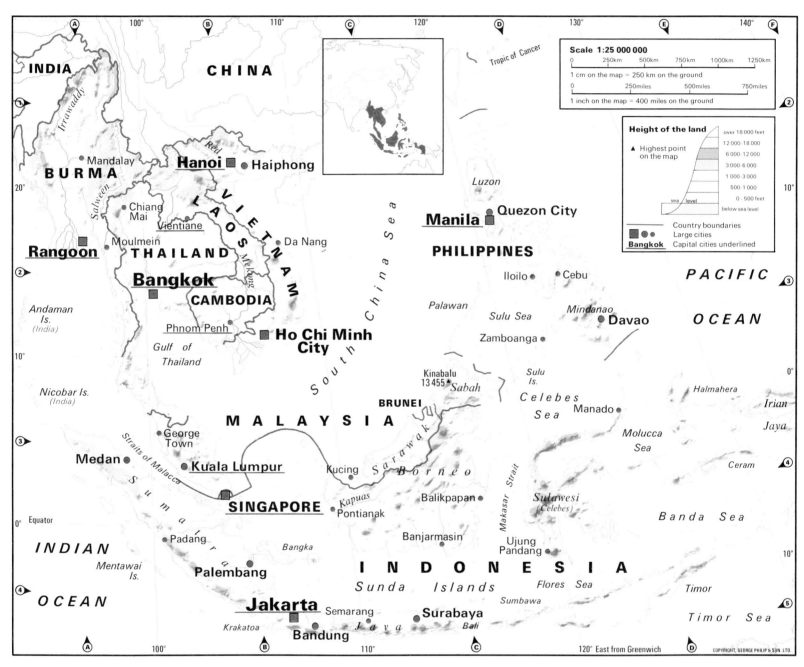

INDIA
CHINA
Tropic of Cancer

Scale 1:25 000 000
0   250km   500km   750km   1000km   1250km
1 cm on the map = 250 km on the ground
0   250miles   500miles   750miles
1 inch on the map = 400 miles on the ground

Height of the land
over 18 000 feet
12 000-18 000
▲ Highest point   6 000-12 000
  on the map   3 000-6 000
                  1 000-3 000
                  500-1 000
sea level   0 - 500 feet
                  below sea level

Country boundaries
Large cities
Bangkok Capital cities underlined

Irrawaddy
Mandalay
BURMA
Hanoi ■ Haiphong
Red
20°
Luzon
Chiang Mai
Moulmein Vientiane Da Nang
Rangoon THAILAND LAOS VIETNAM
Manila ■ Quezon City
PHILIPPINES
Salween
Bangkok
CAMBODIA
Mekong
Iloilo ● ● Cebu
Andaman Is. (India)
Phnom Penh
Ho Chi Minh City
Palawan
Mindanao ● Davao
Sulu Sea
Zamboanga ●
Gulf of Thailand
South China Sea
OCEAN
PACIFIC
Nicobar Is. (India)
Kinabalu 13 455 ▲ Sabah
Sulu Is.
Halmahera
Irian Jaya
BRUNEI
Celebes Sea
Manado ●
MALAYSIA
Sarawak
George Town
Borneo
Molucca Sea
Straits of Malacca
Kucing
Ceram
Medan ●
Kuala Lumpur
Sumatra
Balikpapan ●
Sulawesi (Celebes)
Kapuas
Makasar Strait
Banda Sea
SINGAPORE Pontianak
Padang
Banjarmasin
Ujung Pandang ●
Equator
Bangka
Mentawai Is.
INDIAN
Palembang
INDONESIA
Flores Sea
Timor
Sunda Islands
Sumbawa
OCEAN
Jakarta Semarang Surabaya
Timor Sea
Krakatoa Bandung Java Bali

120° East from Greenwich
COPYRIGHT, GEORGE PHILIP & SON, LTD.

Stamps from Southeast Asia.

Singapore has four main religions:

Christian   Buddhist   Islamic   Hindu
church   temple   mosque   temple

Laos. Elephants carry huge logs
from the jungle. Laos was once
called Lanxang – 'land of a million
elephants.'

Vietnam. Children learn to draw
their country. North and South
Vietnam were united in 1976 after
many years of fighting.

The Equator crosses Southeast Asia, so it is always hot. Heavy tropical rainstorms are common, too.

The mainland and most of the islands are very mountainous. The mountains are covered with thick tropical forest (look at the stamp of Laos). These areas are very difficult to reach and have few people. The large rivers are important routes inland. Their valleys and deltas are very crowded indeed.

Indonesia is the biggest country. It used to be the Dutch East Indies.

The Philippines is another large group of islands, south of China. They were Spanish until 1898.

Malaysia includes part of the mainland and most of northern Borneo.

Singapore is an island at the tip of mainland Malaysia, but a separate country. Both countries were British and Singapore still belongs to the Commonwealth.

Burma was part of the Indian Empire. It became independent in 1948.

Vietnam, Laos and **Cambodia** were once called French Indo-China. The full name of Laos is written in French on the stamp.

Thailand has always been independent, and has a king. It used to be called Siam.

Floating market in Thailand.
Farmers bring their fruit and vegetables to Bangkok market by boat. On some boats there are fish which are cooked on the boat and sold for lunch.

▽

△
Harvesting rice. *Rice grows on terraces cut into the mountainside in Bali. Each terrace is sown and harvested by hand. Bali is a small island east of Java. Some people claim that it is the most beautiful island of Indonesia, and all the world!*

A Thai schoolbook. *This page from a children's book about Thailand shows a man harvesting pineapples. Can you see how he waters the fields from the river?*

▽

Fact box: Indonesia

Did you know that Indonesia: has the **fifth largest population** in the world (see page 9); is the **world's greatest archipelago** – a group of 13,000 islands, which stretches for 3479 miles; has **more active volcanoes** than any other country (77); suffered the **world's biggest recorded bang** – when the island of Krakatoa blew up in a volcanic eruption in 1883.

ประเทศ ไทย ของ ฉัน มี ต้น ข้าว มี ต้น ผัก และ มี ต้น ผลไม้ มาก มาย

In Thailand we have plenty of rice, vegetables and fruit.

CHINA
AND NEIGHBORS

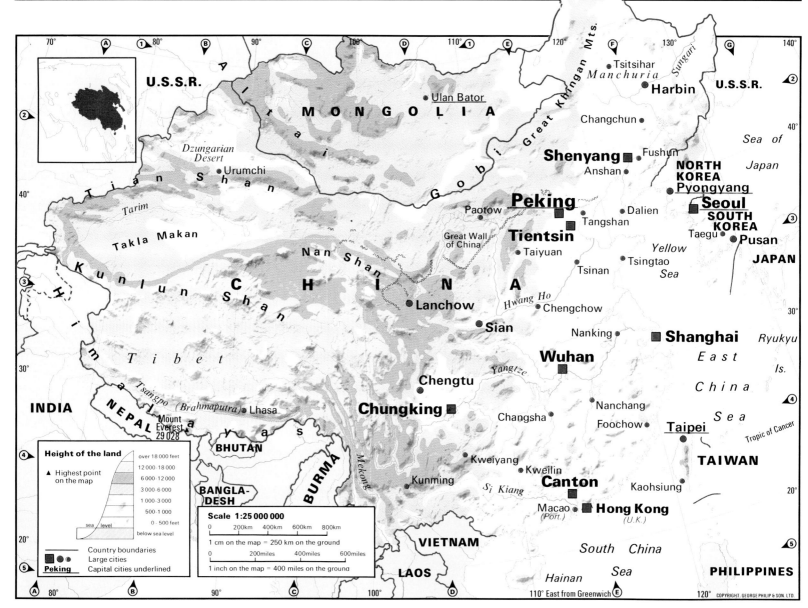

China's amazing mountains. *Both the stamp and the photograph show the amazing shapes of the limestone mountains in southern China. The mountains that look 'unreal' in Chinese paintings really are real! It is almost impossible to travel through this area except by boat. The heavy rain has slowly dissolved the limestone to make these picturesque mountains. They are now one of China's main tourist attractions. The river is the Kwei which flows through Kweilin, an old city dating back to the sixth century.*

China has over a billion people (1,000,000,000) – more than any other country in the world. The map shows that there are many high mountains in China, such as the huge plateau of Tibet and the rugged mountains of the southwest where the Giant Pandas live. Not many people live in these mountains, nor in the deserts of the north, near Mongolia. So the lower land of eastern China is *very* crowded indeed. Rice grows well south of the Yangtze River. North of the Yangtze, where the winters are colder, wheat and corn are important food crops, but it is hard to grow enough.

Building a reservoir. *Everybody, male and female, pulls a heavy cart of rocks to make a new dam across a river. The dam will provide water for power and for irrigation – and it will control flooding too. China has made great progress with projects like this, which use lots of people and few machines. Long ago the Great Wall of China was built in this way to keep out China's enemies.*

China's neighbors

Mongolia is a huge desert country, three times bigger than Spain. It is the world's emptiest country: there are fewer than 3 million people.

North Korea is a communist country. It separated from South Korea in 1945

South Korea has over 43 million people – more than Canada and Australia put together!

Taiwan is an island country which used to be called Formosa, or nationalist China. It is not communist and is not part of the rest of China.

Hong Kong will be a British colony until 1997, when the land will be handed back to China. Big new skyscrapers stand on the hills to fit 6 million people into a crowded island. The hydrofoil is going to **Macao**, a nearby Portuguese colony.

Traffic in Tientsin. *Rush hour in Chinese cities is not the same as in New York or London: there are hardly any cars. People travel on foot, or by bicycle or bus. Tientsin is a big port in northern China and is one of the largest cities in the country.*

Fact box

* One person out of every five people in the world is Chinese.

* This century's worst earthquake happened in Tangshan in 1976. This is in the crowded part of China, so many people were killed.

* The Chinese invented an earthquake detector 1800 years ago. They also invented the compass, paper and printing.

*The place farthest from the open sea is in China: the Dzungarian Desert, 1490 miles from the sea. A man from Norwich in England who cycled there said it is 'hot and horrible'!

* The highest plateau in the world is Tibet. Its average height is nearly 16,400 feet above sea level – as high as Mont Blanc (see page 27)! Lhasa, Tibet, has the world's highest airport, at 14,315 feet. The runway is extra long as there is so little air pressure to help aircraft take off.

* The Chinese language has many dialects: the commonest is Mandarin. Each sound has four tones; words are written using thousands of different characters. Chinese used to be written from top to bottom of the page; now it is written from left to right.

JAPAN

Bullet train. *Japan's 'bullet trains' go like a bullet from a gun! The trains run on new tracks with no sharp curves to slow them down. They provide a superb service except when there is an earthquake warning. When that happens, the trains have to go more slowly, to be safe.*

Japan is quite a small country: it is smaller than France or Spain. Canada is twenty-seven times as big as Japan! But Japan has a big population – about 124,000,000. This is over twice as many people as France, and five times as many as Canada.

People talk of the 'Japanese miracle'. This small country is mostly mountains, has very few mines and hardly any oil, yet it has become the world's biggest producer of televisions, radios, stereos, cameras, trucks, ships and many other things. Japanese cars and computers are admired throughout the world. There are booming cities in the south of Japan, with highly skilled, hardworking people. But most of Japan is still peaceful and beautiful.

In the south rice is the main food crop. Some of the hillsides look like giant steps, because they are terraced to make flat fields for growing rice.

Mount Fuji in winter. *Fujiyama (Mount Fuji) is Japan's most famous mountain. It is an old volcano, 12,388 feet high. In winter, the upper slopes are snow-covered. The 'bullet trains' pass Mount Fuji on their high-speed journey from Tokyo to Nagoya and Osaka.*

Huge baskets for live fish. *Fish are caught and then stored in these huge baskets. The Japanese eat more fish than people in any other country, but sadly the seas near Japan have been polluted by industry. Big Japanese trawlers now fish thousands of miles away from home.*

Many mountains are volcanoes. There are 54 active volcanoes, and over 100 others (see below). The northernmost island, Hokkaido, is much less crowded. It has very cold winters, and even the summers are too cold for growing rice.

Horyu Temple, at Nara

The beautiful temple on the right is called a pagoda. Japanese pagodas are carefully preserved. Their unusual shape originally came partly from Indian temples and partly from Chinese temples. This is one of many Japanese stamps on the theme of national treasures. You could collect them.

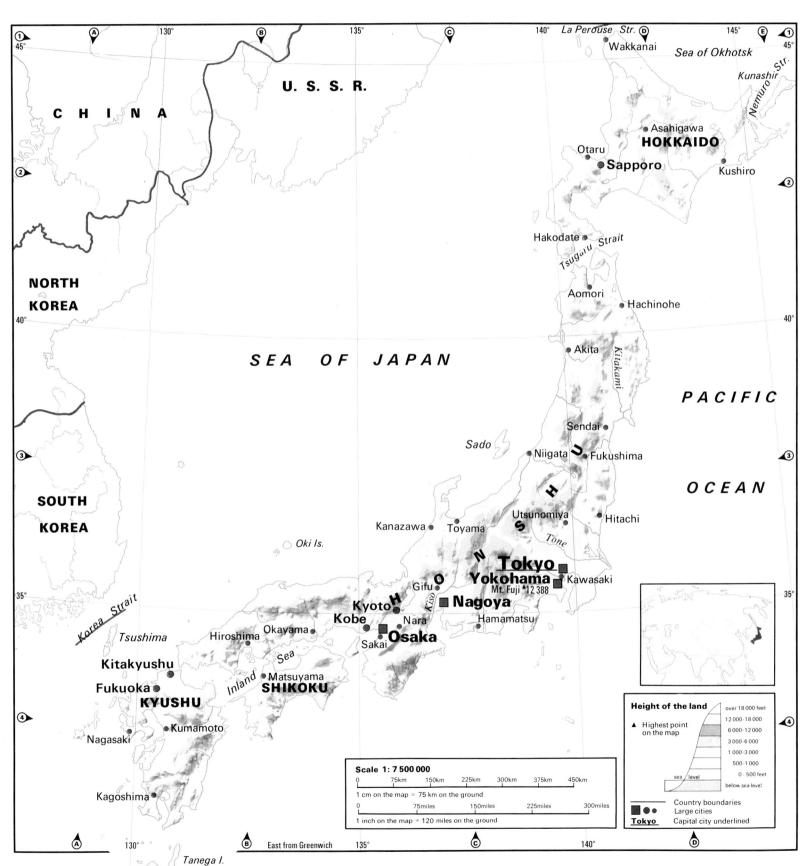

SEA OF OKHOTSK

U.S.S.R.

CHINA

NORTH KOREA

SOUTH KOREA

SEA OF JAPAN

PACIFIC OCEAN

Wakkanai

Asahigawa
HOKKAIDO
Otaru
Sapporo
Kushiro

Hakodate
Tsugaru Strait

Aomori
Hachinohe

Akita
Kitakami

Sendai
Sado
Niigata
Fukushima

H O N S H U

Kanazawa
Toyama
Utsunomiya
Hitachi
Tone

Tokyo
Yokohama
Kawasaki
Mt. Fuji ▲12 388

Gifu
Nagoya
Kyoto
Kobe
Nara
Hamamatsu
Osaka
Sakai

Oki Is.

Hiroshima
Okayama
Inland Sea
Matsuyama
SHIKOKU

Kitakyushu
Fukuoka
KYUSHU
Kumamoto
Nagasaki

Kagoshima

Tsushima
Korea Strait

La Perouse Str.
Kunashir Str.
Nemuro Str.

Tanega I.

Height of the land

	over 18 000 feet
▲ Highest point on the map	12 000-18 000
	6 000-12 000
	3 000-6 000
	1 000-3 000
	500-1 000
sea level	0 · 500 feet
	below sea level

▪ ●● Large cities
Tokyo Capital city underlined
▪ Country boundaries

Scale 1: 7 500 000

0   75km   150km   225km   300km   375km   450km
1 cm on the map = 75 km on the ground

0   75miles   150miles   225miles   300miles
1 inch on the map = 120 miles on the ground

East from Greenwich

AFRICA

◁ **Children in Ghana.** *Everywhere in Africa, there are lots of children. The fathers of these children are fishermen: in the background you can see big dugout canoes. The canoes are made from the huge trees of the rain forest, and can cope with big waves in the Gulf of Guinea. These children get plenty of fish to eat, but in some parts of Africa hunger is a major problem.*

Most of the countries of Africa have quite small populations – except for Nigeria and Egypt. But everywhere, the population is growing fast. It is difficult to provide enough schools and clinics for all the children and there are not enough good jobs. So African countries are trying hard to improve fishing, mining and industry.

Fact box: Africa

Area 11,706,165 square miles

Highest point Mount Kilimanjaro (Tanzania), 19,341 feet

Lowest point Shores of Lake Assal (Djibouti), 508 feet below sea level

Longest river Nile, 4145 miles (also a *world* record)

Largest lake Lake Victoria (East Africa), 26,828 square miles

Biggest country Sudan, 967,494 square miles

Smallest country *Mainland:* Gambia, 4361 square miles; *islands:* Seychelles, 118 square miles (find them on the map on page 9)

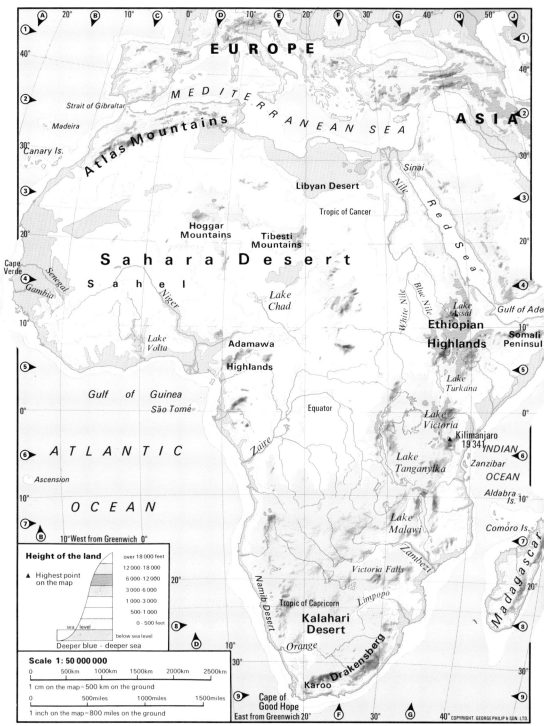

52

The pyramids of Egypt. *The pyramids are tombs which were built by slaves over 4000 years ago. They are* still *the biggest buildings in the whole of Africa. They are near the Nile River, in the Sahara desert.*

These camels are for the tourists that visit the pyramids.

Imagine traveling southwards across Africa, along the 20°E line of longitude. You start in Libya. Your first 600 miles will be across the great Sahara Desert (where you *must* travel in winter) – sand, rock and the high, rugged Tibesti Mountains. Then you reach thorn bushes, in the semi-desert Sahel area of Chad.

By 15°N you are into savanna – very long grass and scattered trees. You cross the country known as CAR for short. The land becomes greener and at about 5°N you reach the equatorial rain forest . . . a real jungle! You are now in Zaïre.

Then the same story happens in reverse – savanna in Angola; then semi-desert (the Kalahari and the Karoo). Finally you reach the mountains and coast of South Africa – a journey of nearly 5000 miles.

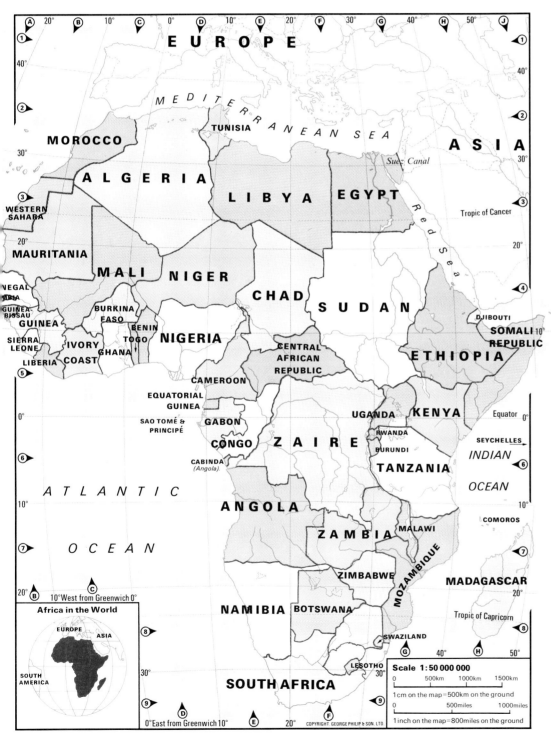

Where do the country names come from?

Ghana, Benin, Mali
Names of great empires in West Africa a long time ago

Gambia, Niger, Nigeria
From big rivers in these countries

Chad From Lake Chad

Namibia From the *Namib* Desert

Tanzania From *Tang*anyika (the mainland) and the island of *Zanz*ibar

Sierra Leone 'Lion Mountain' in Portuguese (named by explorers)

Ivory Coast Ivory, from the tusks of elephants, used to be traded along this coast

NORTH AFRICA

Most of North Africa is desert – but not all. The coastlines and mountains of northwest Africa get winter rain: good crops are grown, and the area is popular all year with tourists from Europe. These countries are Islamic. **Morocco** has the oldest university in the world: the Islamic University in Fez.

Oil has made **Libya** rich. The other countries still have much poverty. The Sahel states, at the southern edge of the Sahara, are among the poorest countries in the world. They had severe famines in the 1970s and 1980s.

Egypt has the biggest population of any North African country. Its capital, Cairo, is one of the biggest cities in the world. The Nile River brings water to the valley and delta. The land is carefully farmed (with irrigation) and crowded with people; the rest of Egypt is almost empty. The map shows that part of the desert is *below* sea level.

The lack of rain has helped to preserve many of the marvelous monuments, palaces and tombs built by the ancient Egyptians. The pyramids at Giza, near Cairo, are 4500 years old (see page 53). They are the only one of the Seven Wonders of the ancient world still surviving.

◁ **Oasis, Algeria.** *The water allows date palms to grow well. But in the background, great sand dunes loom on the skyline: if they advance, they may cover the oasis one day. In the foreground there is rock desert – that is more common than sand desert.*

Huge sand dunes, Libya. *Land-Rover tracks can be seen in the foreground. But no vehicles can cross the huge, steep sand dunes in the background. The Land-Rover has stopped in front of the dunes. Only about a tenth of the Sahara Desert is made up of sand dunes. Other parts are gravel desert, rock desert, salt desert, dried-up lakes and desert mountains.*
▽

△
Camels at market, Tunisia. *Camels are ideal for deserts: they can survive for a long time without water, by relying on the fat in their humps. They can carry heavy loads, and can walk well on soft sand. But nowadays, trucks are taking over from camels for long-distance travel.*

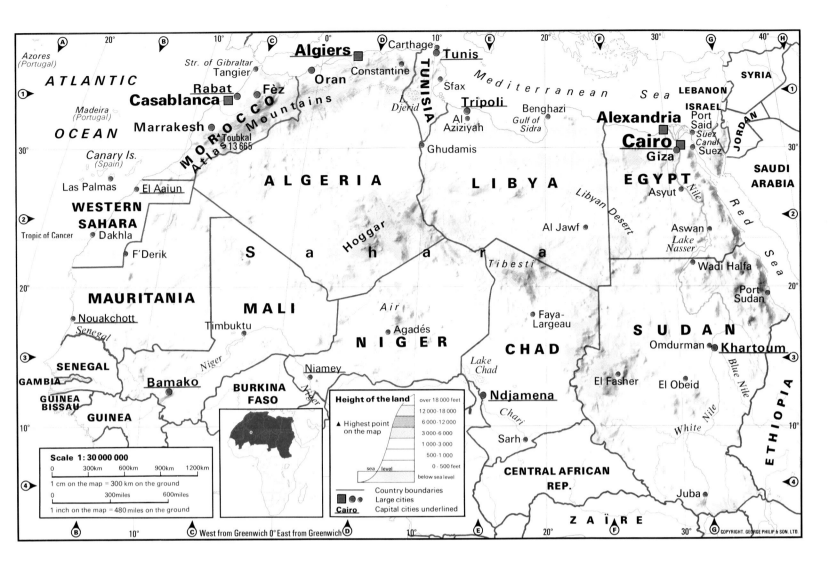

Puzzle picture

This is a satellite photograph of part of the Sahara Desert in southern Libya. Who has drawn these circles in the desert, and why? How have they become green? Why are some circles more green than others?

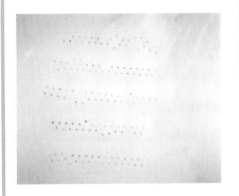

Have a guess – then turn to page 96.

The Suez Canal. *This container ship is traveling through the desert of Egypt! The Suez Canal was dug in 1859–69 by Arabs, organized by a Frenchman, Ferdinand de Lesseps. Before the canal was dug, the route from Europe to India and the Far East went around Africa.*

For almost a century, the canal was a very important route; but now airplanes have taken over almost all the passenger traffic, and many oil tankers are much too big to go through it. Today it is mostly used for freight traveling from Asia to Europe.

Saharan records

The Sahara is the **biggest desert** in the world. It is over 3 million square miles in size. From west to east it is over 3000 miles wide; from north to south it extends about 1200 miles and it is still growing.

The **hottest shade temperature** ever recorded, 136.4°F, was in Al Aziziyah, Libya, in 1922.

The **sunniest** place in the world, over 4300 hours of sunshine per year, is in the eastern Sahara.

The **highest sand dunes** in the world, 1410 feet high, are in east central Algeria (twice as high as the highest point in Denmark).

The **longest river** in the world is the Nile River, 4145 miles. (How strange that a desert should have the world's longest river!)

WEST AFRICA

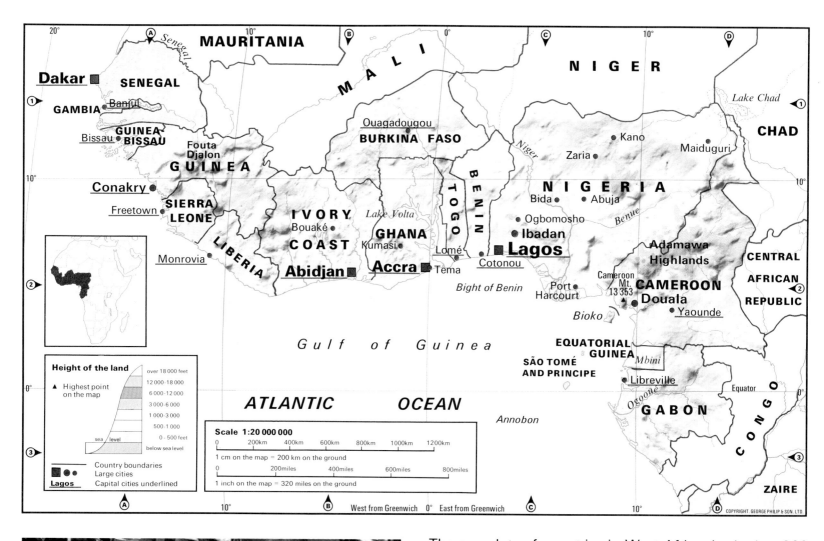

Height of the land
over 18 000 feet
12 000-18 000
6 000-12 000
3 000-6 000
1 000-3 000
500-1 000
0 - 500 feet
below sea level

▲ Highest point on the map

Country boundaries
■ ● ● Large cities
Lagos Capital cities underlined

Scale 1:20 000 000
0   200km   400km   600km   800km   1000km   1200km
1 cm on the map = 200 km on the ground
0   200miles   400miles   600miles   800miles
1 inch on the map = 320 miles on the ground

West from Greenwich 0° East from Greenwich

COPYRIGHT. GEORGE PHILIP & SON. LTD.

There are lots of countries in West Africa. In the last 300 years, European countries grabbed parts of the coastline and later they took over the inland areas as well. Now, all the countries are independent, but still use the language of those who once ruled them. English, French, Spanish or Portuguese is spoken. Many Africans speak a European language as well as one or more African languages. Nigeria is the largest and most populated country in West Africa. It has over 100 million people – more than any other African country. Although English is the official language, there are about 240 others in Nigeria!

◁ **Market day.** *Red peppers for sale in Bida, Nigeria. Red peppers are very popular in West Africa – they give a strong flavor in cooking. Markets are important in both towns and villages in all the countries of West Africa. Most of the selling is done by women.*

Puzzle picture

Why is this man building all these mounds? Make a guess – then turn to page 96.

◁**Extinct volcanoes.** *Long ago these mountains in Cameroon were volcanoes. Now only the cores of the volcanoes are left: the rest has been eroded away. Notice the thatched roofs of the houses.*

Everywhere in West Africa there is rapid progress. Most children now go to primary school, and the capital cities have televisions and airports. But many people are still very poor.

The southern part of West Africa, near the Equator, is forested. The tall trees are being felled for their hardwood. Many crops are grown in the forest area and sold overseas: cocoa (for chocolate-making in England); coffee, pineapples and bananas (for export to France); rubber (for car and truck tires). The main food crops are root crops, such as cassava and yams.

Further north, the trees thin out and there is savanna. The tall grass with some trees is suitable for cattle farming. There are big herds of cattle, and beautiful leather goods are on sale in the markets. Cotton and groundnuts (peanuts) are grown in the savanna lands. The main food crops are grass-like: rice, corn, sorghum and millet.

Yeji ferry, Ghana. *This big ferry carries trucks, cars, people and their heavy loads across Lake Volta. This man-made lake flooded Ghana's main road to the north. You can see trees that died as the water rose in the new lake.* ▷

Harvesting rice in Ghana. *This* ▷ *view could be in Europe or North America! Huge combine-harvesters are reaping rice on a large farm in northern Ghana. But most farms are very small.*

EAST AND CENTRAL AFRICA

Bus services in Africa

Bus journeys in Africa are exciting, and the fares are very cheap, but many roads are very bumpy!

'Safari' is the Swahili word for 'journey'. This bus ticket is for a journey (safari) in Tanzania from Moshi to Dar es Salaam.

Fishermen, Zaïre. *Each one of these fishing boats is made from a single tree, hollowed out with an axe. They are called dugout canoes – there is no danger of a leak in the boat!*

Picking tea in Nandi province, Kenya. *The tender young leaves are picked by hand and taken to a factory where they will be dried and crushed. Tea grows well in the highlands of East Africa. It is an important export of Kenya.*

Central Africa is mostly lowland, with magnificent trees in the tropical rain forest in Zaïre and Congo. Some timber is used for buildings and canoes (see photograph above left); some is exported. The cleared land can grow many tropical crops.

East Africa is mostly high savanna land with long grass and scattered trees. Small parts are reserved for wild animals (see opposite page); in other parts, there are large farms for export crops such as coffee and tea. But in most of East Africa, the people keep cattle and grow crops for their own needs.

The Somali Republic, Djibouti, northern Kenya, and northern Ethiopia are desert areas.

The Masai people *live mainly by herding cattle on the plains near the border of Kenya and Tanzania. These teenage boys are dressed as warriors. They learn to hunt and to guard the cattle. A Masai man has been prime minister of Tanzania.*

Ethiopia is largely mountainous. In most years there is plenty of rain, but this can bring floods and wash away the good soil. In 1985, the country had a terrible famine.

In all these countries the population is growing fast, there is much poverty, and people are moving to the cities. But there are also many signs of development: new farm projects, new ports and roads, and new schools.

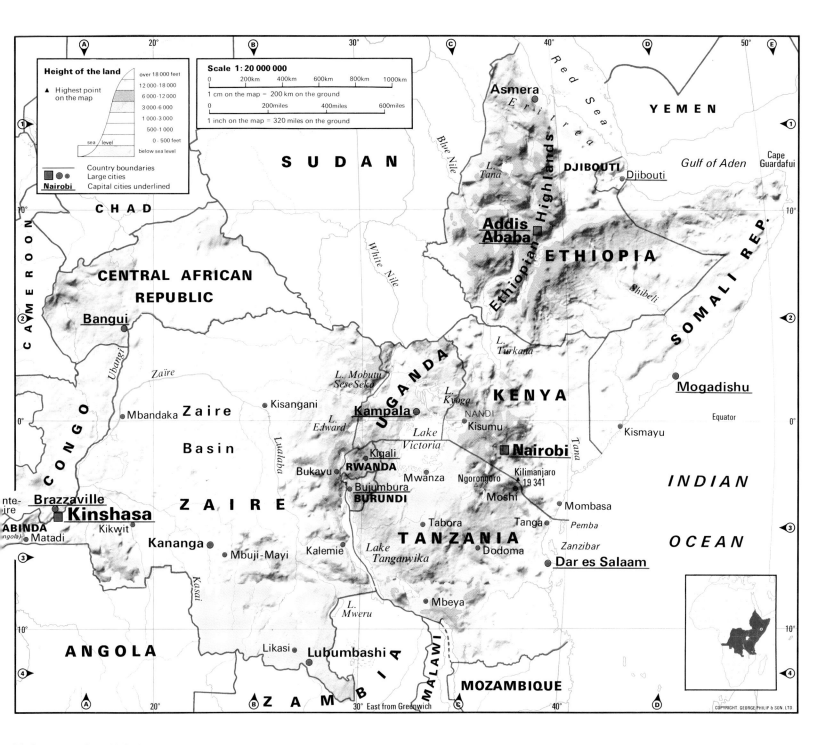

Height of the land

▲ Highest point on the map

over 18 000 feet
12 000-18 000
6 000-12 000
3 000-6 000
1 000-3 000
500-1 000
0 - 500 feet
below sea level

sea level

■ Country boundaries
●●● Large cities
Nairobi Capital cities underlined

Scale 1: 20 000 000

0   200km   400km   600km   800km   1000km

1 cm on the map = 200 km on the ground

0   200miles   400miles   600miles

1 inch on the map = 320 miles on the ground

S U D A N

C H A D

CENTRAL AFRICAN REPUBLIC

C A M E R O O N

Bangui

C O N G O

Ubangi

Zaïre

Mbandaka • **Z a i r e**

• Kisangani

L. Mobutu Sese Seko

B a s i n

Lualaba

Brazzaville
nte-
ire
Kinshasa
ABINDA
ngola) • Matadi   Kikwit •

Kananga •

• Mbuji-Mayi

Z A I R E

Kalemie •

Lake Tanganyika

Likasi •   **Lubumbashi** •

A N G O L A

Z A M B I A

20°   30° East from Greenwich

U G A N D A
L. Edward
Kampala •
Kigali
Bukavu •   **RWANDA**
Bujumbura
BURUNDI

L. Kyoga
NANDI
Kisumu •
Lake Victoria
Mwanza •

Asmera •
Eritrea
L. Tana
Blue Nile

DJIBOUTI
Djibouti •

Addis Ababa ■

Ethiopian Highlands

E T H I O P I A

Shibeli

L. Turkana

K E N Y A

Ngorongoro •   ▲ Kilimanjaro 19 341
Moshi •

• Mombasa

Tanga •
Pemba

White Nile

T A N Z A N I A
• Tabora
Dodoma •
Zanzibar
Dar es Salaam

• Mbeya

L. Mweru

M A L A W I

MOZAMBIQUE

Red Sea

Y E M E N

Gulf of Aden   Cape Guardafui

S O M A L I   R E P.

Mogadishu

Equator
• Kismayu

Tana
■ **Nairobi**

I N D I A N

O C E A N

COPYRIGHT GEORGE PHILIP & SON. LTD.

Zebra and wildebeest *at Ngorongoro, Tanzania. People come from all over the world to go on wildlife safaris in East Africa. This lake is in the crater of an old volcano. Animals gather to drink the water, because there is no other water nearby in the long dry season.*

The game reserves of East Africa are carefully managed to conserve the wildlife. Elephants, lions and giraffes are only 'shot' by cameras now; guns are banned. The money spent by tourists is very important for Kenya and Tanzania.

59

SOUTHERN AFRICA

Most of southern Africa is a high, flat plateau. The rivers cannot be used by ships because of big waterfalls like the Victoria Falls (see page 61). But the rivers can be useful. Two huge dams have been built on the Zambezi River – at Kariba (in Zambia) and at Cabora Bassa (in Mozambique). The map shows the lakes behind each dam. The power of the falling water is used to make electricity.

Angola and **Mozambique** used to be Portuguese colonies, and Portuguese is still their official language – though many different African languages are spoken, too. Most of the other countries shown on the map have English as their official language.

Notice that many southern African countries are landlocked: they have no coastline. The railways leading to the ports in neighboring countries are very important. Copper from Zambia and Botswana and asbestos from Zimbabwe are sent abroad in this way.

The **Republic of South Africa** is the wealthiest country in Africa. It has the richest gold mine in the world, and also priceless diamond mines. But most of the black people are very poor. They have been kept apart from the white people by the government, which is run by white people. This policy is called apartheid.

All the other countries of southern Africa disagree with apartheid – even Lesotho, a country which is completely surrounded by South Africa. Some parts of South Africa have been made into Bantustans – mini-countries which are partly run by Africans. But they are not recognized as real countries by the United Nations, so they are not on our map.

A village in Zambia

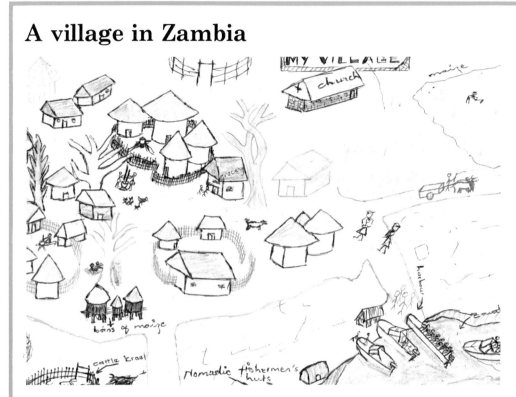

Sianga drew this picture of her village during a lesson at her school in Zambia. Her village is close to the Zambezi River in the western part of the country.

An unfriendly notice *in three languages on a white-owned poultry farm in South Africa.*

A baobab tree. *In almost all southern Africa there is a long, hot dry season. The baobab tree is good at surviving a long drought. It has a specially fat trunk and main branches which hold water like a sponge and help to keep it alive.*

World Greats

The **Victoria Falls** (*right*) are on the Zambezi River, at the border of Zambia and Zimbabwe. Africans call the falls *Mosi-oi-tunya* – 'the smoke that thunders'. They were named after the English Queen Victoria by the explorer David Livingstone.

The world's **oldest mines** are in Swaziland. Iron ore was mined here 43,000 years ago.

The world's **deepest mine** is the gold mine at Carletonville, South Africa. It is 12,392 feet deep – and still getting deeper!

The world's **biggest diamond** was found near Pretoria, South Africa, in 1905.

Mining diamonds. *Diamonds are mined in several countries in southern Africa. The huge mine shown here* (above right) *is in*

Namibia. The desert is scraped away to reach the rock beneath, where diamonds are found. The yellow truck is huge, but looks very small in this vast mine.

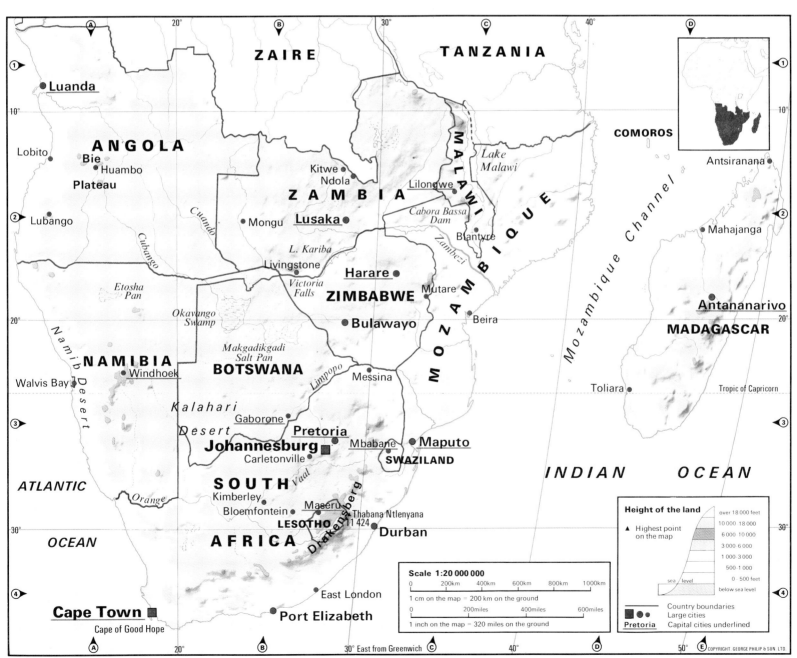

In South Africa, Pretoria is shown as the capital but the parliament meets in Cape Town.

NORTH AMERICA

North America includes many Arctic islands, a huge mainland area (quite narrow in Central America) and the islands in the Caribbean Sea. The map shows the great mountain ranges which are the most impressive feature of this continent. Almost all the west is mountainous; these are mostly fold mountains but the highest peaks are volcanoes. The Appalachian Mountains in the east are also fold mountains. And the island chains of the northwest (the Aleutian Islands) and the southeast (the West Indies) are the tops of underwater ranges.

Fruit market, Barbados, West Indies. *The West Indies have hot sunshine and plenty of rain. This is an ideal climate for growing excellent fruit. Which types of fruit can you recognize in this market? (Answer on page 96.)*

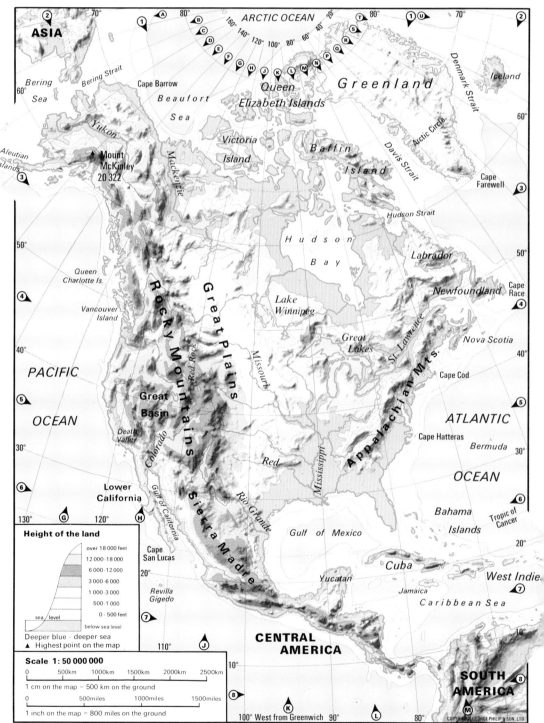

Height of the land

| over 18 000 feet |
| 12 000 - 18 000 |
| 6 000 - 12 000 |
| 3 000 - 6 000 |
| 1 000 - 3 000 |
| 500 - 1 000 |
| 0 - 500 feet |
| below sea level |

Deeper blue - deeper sea
▲ Highest point on the map

Scale 1: 50 000 000

0   500km   1000km   1500km   2000km   2500km

1 cm on the map = 500 km on the ground

0   500miles   1000miles   1500miles

1 inch on the map = 800 miles on the ground

The political map of North America is quite a simple one. The boundary between Canada and the USA is mostly at exactly 49°N. Four of the five Great Lakes have one shore in Canada and one shore in the USA.* Canada's two biggest cities, Toronto and Montreal, are south of the 49° line! Find them on the map on page 65.

The eight countries of Central America have more complicated boundaries. Six of these countries have two coastlines. The map shows that one country has a coastline only on the Pacific Ocean, and one has a coastline only on the Caribbean Sea.* The West Indies are made up of islands and there are lots of countries too. They are shown in more detail on pages 74 and 75.

Greenland was a colony of Denmark until quite recently, but now it is self-governing. Most of Greenland is covered by ice all year.

*Which ones? Answers on page 96.

Fact box: North America

Area 9,362,538 square miles
Highest point Mount McKinley (Alaska), 20,322 feet
Lowest point Death Valley (California), 282 feet below sea level
Longest river Red Rock-Missouri-Mississippi, 3710 miles
Largest lake Lake Superior*, 31,795 square miles
Biggest country Canada, 3,851,788 square miles
Smallest country Grenada (West Indies), 132 square miles
Richest country USA
Poorest country Haiti
Most crowded country Barbados
Least crowded country Canada

*The world's largest *freshwater* lake

Flyovers, Los Angeles, USA.
There are four levels of road at this road junction in Los Angeles, yet there is a traffic jam as well! The USA has more cars than any other country.

CANADA

Coin and flag. *Both the 1-cent coin and the flag show the national emblem of Canada, the maple leaf. In summer, the leaves of the maple tree are green, but in the fall (autumn) the leaves turn bright red. Canada's woodlands are specially beautiful in September and October (see photograph below right).*

Only one country in the world is bigger than Canada*, but thirty countries have more people than Canada. Most of Canada is almost empty: very few people live on the islands of the north, or in the Northwest Territories, or in the western mountains, or near Hudson Bay. The farmland of the prairies (see the stamp) is uncrowded too. So . . . where *do* Canadians live?

The answer is that more Canadians live in cities than in the countryside. The map shows where the biggest cities are – all of them are in the southern part of Canada, and none are as far north as Norway or Sweden in Europe.

The photographs and stamps show Canada in summer. In winter, it is very cold indeed in central and northern Canada. Children go to school even when it is 40° below zero.

*Which country? See pages 38–9.

Languages in Canada

Canada has two official languages: French and English. So the stamps say 'Postes/Postage', instead of only 'Postage'. Most of the French-speaking Canadians live in the province of Quebec.

The biggest city in Quebec is Montreal: it is four times as big as Ottawa, the capital of Canada.

A long-distance train, *with diesel engines and silver coaches, crosses a viaduct in the province of Ontario. It is 2857 miles from Montreal to Vancouver by train. A hundred years ago it was the trans-Canada railway that helped to unite Canada as one country.*

▽

Canadian contrasts

△ This stamp is an air picture of the prairies of central Canada. The huge flat fields of grain reach to the far horizon, and beyond. The only big buildings are grain elevators, for storing the harvested wheat.

In western Canada, the Rocky Mountains are high and jagged. There are glaciers among the peaks.

▽

△

The Niagara Falls *are between Lake Erie and Lake Ontario, on the border of the USA and Canada. The tourists on the boat may get soaked by the spray! Big ships have to use a canal, with locks, to get past the falls.*

How to remember the five Great Lakes

Try using the first letters of the Great Lakes to make a sentence.

Superior	Super
Michigan	Man
Huron	Helps
Erie	Every
Ontario	One

Now you'll *never* forget the west-to-east order of the Great Lakes!

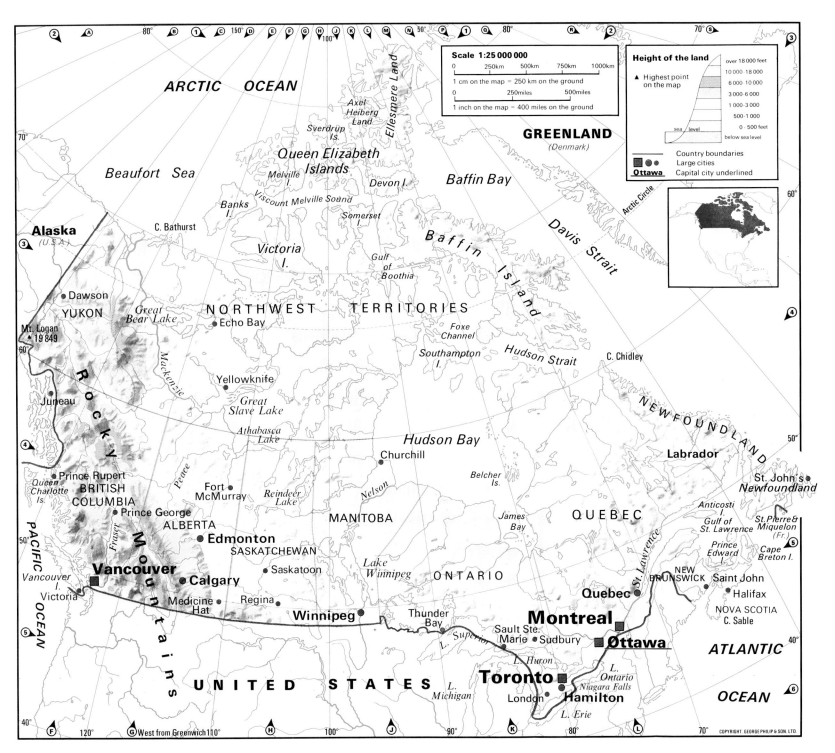

ARCTIC OCEAN

GREENLAND
(Denmark)

Scale 1:25 000 000
0   250km   500km   750km   1000km
1 cm on the map = 250 km on the ground
0   250miles   500miles
1 inch on the map = 400 miles on the ground

Height of the land
▲ Highest point on the map

over 18 000 feet
10 000-18 000
6 000-10 000
3 000-6 000
1 000-3 000
500-1 000
0-500 feet
sea level
below sea level

Country boundaries
Large cities
Ottawa Capital city underlined

Axel Heiberg Land

Ellesmere Land

Sverdrup Is.

Beaufort Sea

Queen Elizabeth Islands

Melville I.

Devon I.

Baffin Bay

Banks I.

Viscount Melville Sound

Somerset I.

C. Bathurst

Victoria I.

Gulf of Boothia

Baffin Island

Davis Strait

Arctic Circle

Alaska (U.S.A.)

Dawson

YUKON

Great Bear Lake

Echo Bay

NORTHWEST TERRITORIES

Foxe Channel

Mt. Logan ▲ 19 849

Yellowknife

Southampton I.

Hudson Strait

C. Chidley

Juneau

Great Slave Lake

NEWFOUNDLAND

Athabasca Lake

Hudson Bay

Labrador

Churchill

Prince Rupert

Queen Charlotte Is.

BRITISH COLUMBIA

Fort McMurray

Reindeer Lake

Belcher Is.

St. John's Newfoundland

Prince George

Nelson

ALBERTA

MANITOBA

James Bay

QUEBEC

Anticosti I.

Gulf of St. Lawrence

St. Pierre & Miquelon (Fr.)

Prince Edward I.

Cape Breton I.

Fraser

Edmonton

SASKATCHEWAN

Lake Winnipeg

ONTARIO

St. Lawrence

NEW BRUNSWICK

Saint John

Vancouver

Saskatoon

Calgary

Halifax

Vancouver I.

Victoria

Medicine Hat

Regina

Quebec

NOVA SCOTIA

C. Sable

PACIFIC OCEAN

Winnipeg

Thunder Bay

Montreal

ROCKY Mountains

Sault Ste. Marie

Sudbury

Øttawa

ATLANTIC

L. Superior

Toronto

L. Huron

L. Ontario

Niagara Falls

Hamilton

UNITED STATES

L. Michigan

London

L. Erie

OCEAN

West from Greenwich

COPYRIGHT. GEORGE PHILIP & SON. LTD.

◁ **Montreal: old and new.** *The old houses have been pulled down to make way for huge new office blocks. Three million people live in Montreal.*

The St Lawrence. *This big ship is passing islands in the St Lawrence River. The ship is going from the Great Lakes to the Atlantic Ocean. A seaway with huge locks has been built to bypass the rapids, shallows and waterfalls on parts of the river.* ▷

USA

Alaska is the biggest state of the USA – but it has the fewest people. It was bought from Russia in 1867 for seven million dollars: the best bargain ever, particularly as oil was discovered a hundred years later. Oil has helped Alaska to become rich. Fish and timber are the other main products. Much of Alaska is mountainous or covered in forest. In the north, there is darkness all day in December, and months of ice-cold weather.

Flag of Alaska. *The flag of Alaska shows stars in the northern sky known as the 'plough' or the 'big dipper.' At the top right is the Pole Star: this reminds us that Alaska is in the far north. The flag was chosen in a competition; the winner was only 13 years old.*

These are 48 of the 50 states.
The other two are Alaska (map above) and Hawaii (map below).
⭐ State capital

ABBREVIATIONS
VT. = Vermont
N.H. = New Hampshire
MASS. = Massachusetts
CONN. = Connecticut
D.C. = District of Columbia

Hawaii *is the newest state in the USA: it became a state in 1959. Honolulu is on Oahu island.*
These faraway Pacific islands are the tops of volcanoes, over 1800 miles from mainland USA (see the map on page 83). If the height of Mauna Kea is measured from the seabed, it is 32,883 feet, the tallest mountain in the world.

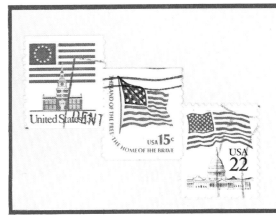

Stars and stripes

In 1776 there were only 13 states in the USA; so the US flag had 13 stars and 13 stripes. As more and more states joined the USA, more stars were added to the flag. Now there are 50 states, and 50 stars. But the 13 stripes on today's flag still recall the original 13 states.

The maps show the 50 states of the USA. The first 13 states were all on the East Coast: these states were settled by Europeans who had sailed across the Atlantic (see the photograph of a pilgrim ship on page 69).

As the Americans moved westward, so more and more states were formed. The Western states are bigger than the states in the East. You can see their straight boundaries on the map.

Who are 'the Americans'?

Out of every 100 people in the USA, 83 have ancestors from Europe. Colonists came from Britain to the Eastern states, from France to the Southern states, and from Spain to the Pacific coastline in the West. Later on,

people came from almost all parts of Europe to the USA. About 12 people out of every 100 came from West Africa, brought to the USA as slaves to work in the Southern states. By 1865, the slaves were free. Many black Americans now live in the northeast USA. More recently, many Spanish-speaking people have entered the USA from Mexico and from Puerto Rico in the Caribbean.

There are fewer than one million American Indians now, some of whom live on special 'reservations.'

5-cent coin. E PLURIBUS UNUM *on this coin is Latin for 'Out of many – one': many peoples have come together to become one country. This 5-cent piece is called a nickel.*

State flags. *Each state has its own flag and some of them tell you about the history of the state.*

Wyoming *has a buffalo in the center of its flag because this state was part of the Wild West where buffaloes used to roam freely.*

Mississippi *has the French flag (red, white and blue stripes) because it belonged to France until 1803.*

The cross at top left was used as a flag by the Southern states in the Civil War in 1861–65.

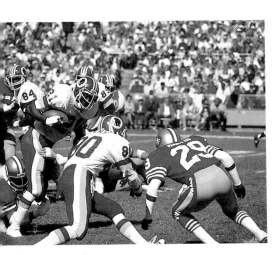

Football. *The Washington Redskins play the San Francisco 49ers. The team from the West Coast has traveled 2800 miles for this game. The players travel by air – it takes three days to cross the USA by train!*

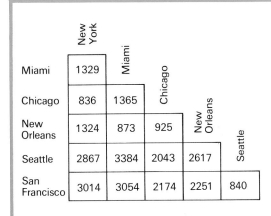

	New York	Miami	Chicago	New Orleans	Seattle
Miami	1329				
Chicago	836	1365			
New Orleans	1324	873	925		
Seattle	2867	3384	2043	2617	
San Francisco	3014	3054	2174	2251	840

Road distances in miles

Distance chart

Read the chart just like a table chart, or a graph. The distance chart shows how big the USA is. In fact, New York is nearer to London, England, than it is to San Francisco! How far is it from Seattle to Miami? New Orleans to Chicago? (Find these places on the maps on pages 68–71.) (Answers on page 96.)

EASTERN USA

Which US city is most important?

Washington is the capital city, where the President lives. But *New York* has far more people and industries than Washington. So *both* are the most important city – but in different ways.

The map shows only half the USA, but over three-quarters of the population live in this half of the country.

The great cities of the Northeast were the first big industrial areas in America. Pittsburgh's football team is still called the Pittsburgh Steelers, even though many of the steelworks have closed down.

In recent years, many people have moved from the 'snow belt' of the North to the 'sun belt' of the South. New industries are booming in the South, where once there was much poverty. And many older people retire to Florida, where even midwinter feels almost like summer.

The Appalachian Mountains are beautiful, especially in the fall (autumn), when the leaves of the trees turn red. But this area is the poorest part of the USA. Coal mines have closed and farmland is poor. The good farmland is west of the Appalachians, where you can drive for hundreds of miles past fields of wheat and sweet corn. In the South it is hot enough for cotton, tobacco and peanuts to be successful crops.

Plan for better cities!

Turn the book clockwise and you will see patios, parks and gardens among the skyscrapers!

Washington, DC. *There is a world of difference between the well-kept rich suburbs* (above) *and the run-down slum area* (right) *of Washington, DC, the capital city of the USA.*

Manhattan Island, New York. *The world's first skyscrapers were built on Manhattan Island: the hard granite rock gave good foundations. The older skyscrapers each have a different shape; the newer ones are flat-topped.*

Plantation-owner's house in Virginia. *Plantation owners grew rich from tobacco and cotton. They lived in fine houses like this one. But their slaves lived in very poor houses.*

Winter in Pittsburgh. *Winter in the northern USA can be very cold indeed. But these Pittsburgh children are enjoying the fresh, crisp snow, before it becomes polluted by smoke from the steelworks and factories.*

The Earth from the moon

This is the view that American astronauts saw from the moon. Half the Earth is in darkness. Neil Armstrong of the USA was the first man on the moon, July 21, 1969.

Pilgrim ship, New England. *The Pilgrim Fathers sailed to America in 1620 from England to start a new life. In 1957 a replica pilgrim ship was built and sailed to America.*

Puzzle stamp

Which river is this? Where does it flow to? And why is it called 'Great River Road'? (Answer on page 96.)

Map

Scale 1:20 000 000

0   200km   400km   600km   800km
1 cm on the map = 200 km on the ground
0   200miles   400miles
1 inch on the map = 320 miles on the ground

Height of the land

▲ Highest point on the map

over 18 000 feet
12 000 - 18 000
6 000 - 12 000
3 000 - 6 000
1 000 - 3 000
500 - 1 000
sea / level   0 - 500 feet
below sea level

Country boundaries
Large cities
Washington Capital city underlined
For the states of the U.S.A. see page 66

CANADA

Lake Superior
Fargo
Duluth
Minneapolis
St. Paul
Mississippi
Sioux Falls
Milwaukee
L. Michigan
Lake Huron
Detroit
Chicago
Toledo
Lake Erie
Cleveland
L. Ontario
Albany
Buffalo
Boston
C. Cod
Providence
Omaha
Missouri
Pittsburgh
New York
Indianapolis
Columbus
Philadelphia
Baltimore
Washington
Kansas City
Cincinnati
Ohio
Richmond
St. Louis
Louisville
Norfolk
Wichita
Nashville
Mt. Mitchell
6.683
Charlotte
Tulsa
Arkansas
Memphis
Tennessee
Chattanooga
ATLANTIC
Oklahoma City
Red
Atlanta
Birmingham
Charleston
OCEAN
Fort Worth
Dallas
Montgomery
Austin
Baton Rouge
Jacksonville
Houston
San Antonio
New Orleans
C. Canaveral
Tampa
Palm Beach
Everglades
BAHAMAS
Gulf of Mexico
Miami
C. Sable
Key West
COPYRIGHT. GEORGE PHILIP & SON. LTD.
West from Greenwich

Mississippi
Appalachian Mts.
Hudson

WESTERN USA

△

Grand Canyon, Arizona.
The Colorado River has cut a huge canyon a mile deep in this desert area of the USA. The mountains slowly rose, while the river kept digging its valley deeper.

Wheat harvest, USA. *Three huge combine harvesters move across a field of wheat. 150 years ago, this land was covered in grass and grazed by buffaloes. Much of this wheat will go abroad.*

▽

Football

Many of the team names have a meaning that is linked to their city's geography or history.

San Francisco 49ers 1849 was the year of the great Californian Gold Rush, when many people came to look for gold.

Denver Broncos Denver, Colorado, was a center for cowboys in the days of the wild west: 'bucking broncos' were their horses!

Houston Oilers Houston, Texas, became a very wealthy city after oil was discovered.

Seattle Seahawks Seattle, Washington, is on an inlet of the Pacific Ocean.

Do you know any other teams?

△

Rodeo in Montana. *There are few real cowboys nowadays – and trucks are used more than horses. But rodeos are popular with local people – and with tourists. At this junior rodeo at Big Timber, Montana, a young rider is trying to show his skill.*

California

California now has more people in it than any other state in the USA. It has every advantage. In the Central Valley the climate is right for many crops: oranges from California are well-known in the USA and abroad. Grapes grow well, and are made into wine.

The desert of the south is attractive to retired people – many people migrate here from all over the USA.

Many areas on this map have hardly any people. The Rocky Mountains are beautiful for vacations, but it is hard to make a living there. The only big city on the high plateaus west of the Rockies is Salt Lake City, Utah. Some former mining towns are now 'ghost towns': when the mines closed, all the people left. The toughest area of all is the desert land of Arizona in the Southwest. The mountains and deserts were a great problem to the pioneers.

East of the Rockies are the Great Plains. The dry plains have enormous cattle ranches; where there is enough rain, crops of wheat and sweet corn (maize) stretch to the horizon.

The Pacific coastlands of the Northwest have plenty of rain and forestry is important. The climate is quite like northwest Europe.

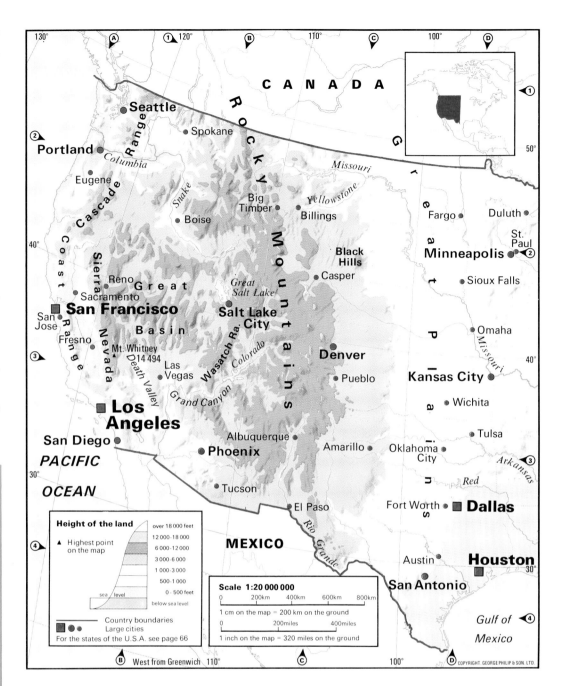

What do the names mean?

The Spanish were the first settlers in the western USA, and they have left us many Spanish names. Here are some:

Amarillo (Texas) ..Yellow
Colorado ....Colored
El Paso
(Texas).................The pass
Los Angeles ....The angels
Las Vegas ....The fertile
(Nevada)   plains
San José..............St Joseph
San Francisco .....St Francis
Sierra Nevada .....Snowy
                        Mountains

Streetcar, San Francisco.
Streetcars still climb the steep hills in San Francisco, California. A moving cable runs beneath the street. The car is fixed to the cable and starts with a jerk! There is a modern 'rapid transit' railway system too – but tourists prefer to see the city from the streetcars.

CENTRAL AMERICA

◁ **Ruins at Chichen Itza, Mexico.** *Great temples were built by the people known as Mayas over a thousand years ago. These amazing ruins are in Yucatan, the most easterly part of Mexico. Today this is an area of jungle, with few people.*

MEXICAN TORTILLAS

A recipe for you to cook
TORTILLAS
Ingredients
8 ounces of maize flour (sweet-corn flour)
salt
water

Recipe
1 Mix the corn flour, salt, and water into a soft dough.
2 Pat into round shapes about $\frac{1}{4}$ inch thick, and $4\frac{1}{2}$ inches across.
3 Melt a little margarine in a frying pan.
4 Place the tortillas in the hot frying pan.
5 For best results, turn the tortillas over.
6 Serve at once!

You have now cooked one of the most important meals of Central America. Maize (sweet corn) was developed as a crop in the Americas, and is now grown in many parts of the world. You eat corn often as cornflakes and macaroni.

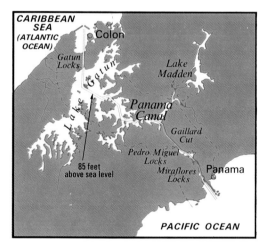

The Panama Canal *links the Caribbean Sea with the Pacific Ocean. It was opened in 1914. Many workers died of fever while digging the canal through the jungle. It is 50 miles long, and the deepest cutting is 269 feet deep – the world's biggest 'ditch'.*

There are six locks along the route of the canal. The photograph (below left) shows three ships in Gatun Lake, 85 feet above sea level (see map). Over 15,000 ships use the canal each year, and sometimes there are 'traffic jams' at the locks: it is the busiest big-ship canal in the world. Before the canal was built, the only sea route from Pacific to Atlantic was around the tip of
◁ *South America.*

Mexico is by far the most important country on this map. Over 82 million people live in Mexico – more than in any country in Europe. Mexico City has a population of about 15 million: it is one of the biggest cities in the world. A major earthquake did great damage there in 1985.

Most Mexicans live on the high plateau of central Mexico. There are very few people in the northern desert, in Lower California in the northwest, in the southern jungle, or in Yucatan in the east.

The other seven countries on this map are quite small. None of them has as many people as Mexico City!

Once ruled by Spain, these countries have been independent since the 1820s. Revolutions and civil wars have caused many problems in Central America. But the climate is good for growing many tropical crops – once the jungle has been cleared.

What do the names mean?

Many names in the countries of Central America are based on Spanish, the official language.

El Salvador The Savior (Jesus Christ)
San José (capital of Costa Rica) St Joseph
Costa Rica The rich coast
Pacific Ocean Peaceful ocean

Guatemala: drying coffee beans. *Coffee berries grow on bushes in tropical countries. The berries are picked, and the seeds taken out and dried in the sun. We call these dried seeds coffee beans.*

The man in the photograph is turning the beans, so that they dry on both sides.

Coffee is the most important export of several Central American countries. Many other tropical crops are exported, including sugar, bananas and pineapple.

WEST INDIES

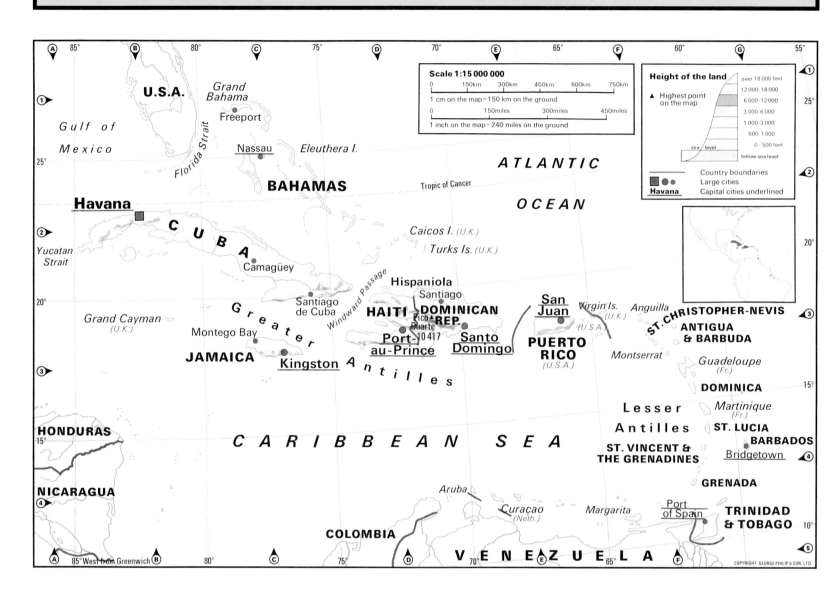

Farming in Jamaica

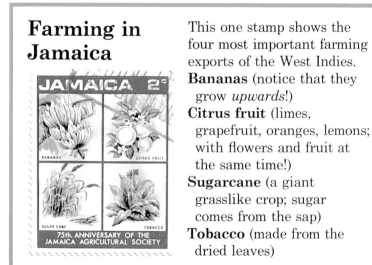

This one stamp shows the four most important farming exports of the West Indies.

Bananas (notice that they grow *upwards*!)

Citrus fruit (limes, grapefruit, oranges, lemons; with flowers and fruit at the same time!)

Sugarcane (a giant grasslike crop; sugar comes from the sap)

Tobacco (made from the dried leaves)

The West Indies are a large group of islands in the Caribbean Sea. Some islands are high and volcanic, others are low coral islands – but all of them are beautiful. Most West Indians have African ancestors: they were brought from West Africa as slaves, to work in the sugar and tobacco fields.

Today most of the islands are independent countries – and tourism is more important than farming in many places. Winter is the best time to visit; summer is very hot and humid, with the risk of hurricanes. In recent years many West Indians have emigrated to Great Britain from Commonwealth islands, to France from Guadeloupe and Martinique, and to the USA from Puerto Rico. A few islands have developed their minerals, for example bauxite in Jamaica and oil in Trinidad.

Coconut palms and beach, Barbados. *It is beautiful – but beware! The tropical sun can quickly burn your skin. And if you seek shade under the coconut palms, you might get hit by a big coconut! Even so, the West Indies are very popular with tourists – especially Americans escaping from cold winters.*

Loading bananas, Dominica. *Bananas are the main export of several islands. Here women are carrying heavy loads of bananas on their heads to the small boats which take the bananas to the Geest banana ship. The bananas travel to Europe in this refrigerated ship. Loading the ship is easier where islands have deep-water harbors.*

Dutch colonial houses, Curaçao. *The island of Curaçao has been Dutch for many years. The colonists came from the Netherlands, and tried to build houses just like the ones at home. Several small West Indian islands still have European connections.*

West Indian variety

In **Cuba**, Spanish is the main language. But Cuba is allied with the USSR, not with Spain: it has a communist government.

St Vincent is part of the Commonwealth and seems very British (but arrowroot and breadfruit only grow in the tropics).

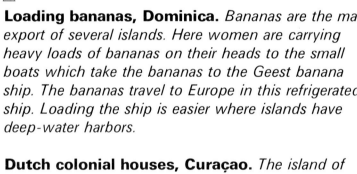

Guadeloupe is not just French – it is officially part of France. This stamp was used in Guadeloupe *and* in all of France!

Curaçao is Dutch: the stamp shows Dutch colonial houses, and the Queen of the Netherlands. Compare the photograph (*right*).

SOUTH AMERICA

◁ **Brasilia, Brazil.** *Brasilia became the new capital of Brazil in 1960. The photograph shows the parliament building on the left, built in concrete and shaped like a bowl, and a tall office block. Most Brazilians live near the coast, and Brasilia was a brave attempt to get people to move inland: it is 620 miles from the sea. Over a million people now live there.*

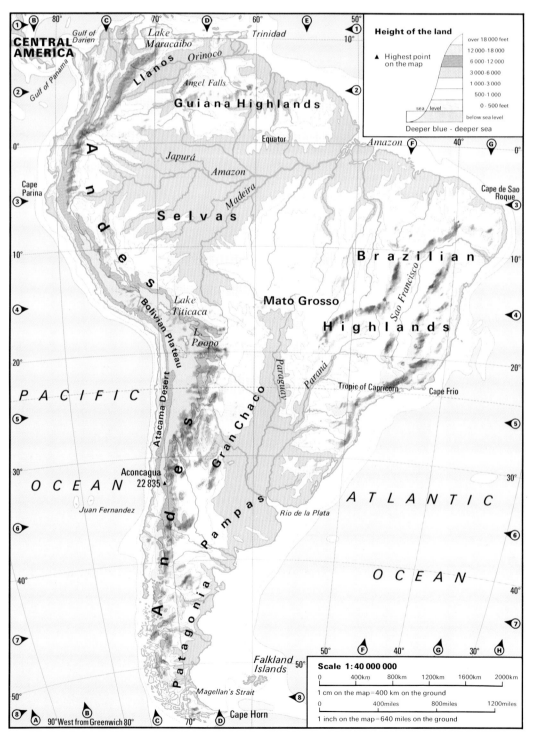

Fact box:
South America

Area 6,795,360 square miles

Highest point Mount Aconcagua (Argentina), 22,835 feet

Lowest point No land below sea level

Longest river Amazon, 4006 miles

Largest lake Lake Titicaca (Bolivia and Peru), 3199 square miles

Biggest country Brazil, 3,286,470 square miles

Smallest country Surinam*, 63,000 square miles

Richest country Venezuela

Poorest country Bolivia

Most crowded country Ecuador

Least crowded country Surinam

*French Guiana is smaller, but it is not independent

Reed boat on Lake Titicaca.
Lake Titicaca is the highest navigable lake in the world: 12,503 feet above sea level. The fishing boat is made of totora reeds which grow around the shores. Bundles of reeds are tied together, and even the sails are made of woven reeds.

The lake is shared between Peru and Bolivia. A steam-powered ferry-boat travels the length of the lake. A river flows southward from Lake Titicaca to Lake Poopo, and then flows onward and vanishes in the high, dry plateau.

Why is Lake Titicaca the only stretch of water available to the Bolivian navy? (Check the map.)

A tour of South America would be very exciting. At the Equator are the hot steamy jungles of the Amazon lowlands. To the west comes the great climb up to the Andes mountains. The peaks are so high that even the volcanoes are snowcapped all year. Travelers on buses and trains are offered extra oxygen to breathe, because the air is so thin.

Squeezed between the Andes and the Pacific Ocean in Peru and northern Chile is the world's driest desert. Farther south in Chile are more wet forests – but these forests are cool. The Chilean pine (monkey puzzle tree) originates here. But eastward, in Argentina, there is less rain and more grass. Cattle on the pampas are rounded up by cowboys, and farther south is the very cold and dry area called Patagonia.

South America stretches farther south than any other continent (apart from Antarctica). The cold and stormy tip of South America, Cape Horn, is only 620 miles from Antarctica.

In every South American country, the population is growing fast. Most of the farmland is owned by a few rich people, and many people are desperately poor. Young people are leaving the countryside for the cities, most of which are encircled by shanty towns.

South America in the World

Scale 1:40 000 000

1 cm on the map = 400 km on the ground

1 inch on the map = 640 miles on the ground

TROPICAL SOUTH AMERICA

Amazon jungle *at the border of Guyana and Brazil. The hot, wet jungle covers thousands of square miles. There is no cool season, and the forest is always green. The trees can be as much as 160 feet high. New roads and villages, mines and dams are being built in the Brazilian jungle.*

The Andean states. Colombia, Ecuador, Peru and Bolivia are known as the Andean states. **Colombia** is known for its coffee. Bananas and other tropical crops grow near the coast of **Ecuador**, but the capital city is high in the mountains. **Peru** relies on mountain rivers to bring water to the dry coastal area.

Bolivia has the highest capital city in the world. It is the poorest country in South America: farming is difficult and even the tin mines hardly make a profit.

East of the Andes, settlers are clearing parts of the forest.

Machu Picchu, Peru, *the lost city of the Incas, is perched on a mountainside 7800 feet above sea level. The last Inca emperor probably lived here in 1580. The ruins were rediscovered in 1911.*

Brazil – the giant. Brazil is by far the biggest country in South America, and has more people than the rest of South America put together (about 150 million).

Most people still live near the coast. Parts of the Amazon forest are now being settled, but large areas inland are still almost empty. The poorest parts are in the northeast, where the rains often fail, and in the shanty-towns around the big cities. Modern industry is growing very fast, but there are still too few jobs. Brazil has pioneered fuel made from sugarcane for cars and trucks.

The llama *is the most important animal in the Andes – it provides milk, meat and leather for these Quechua Indian women. They are following one of the Inca tracks which linked the ancient cities.*

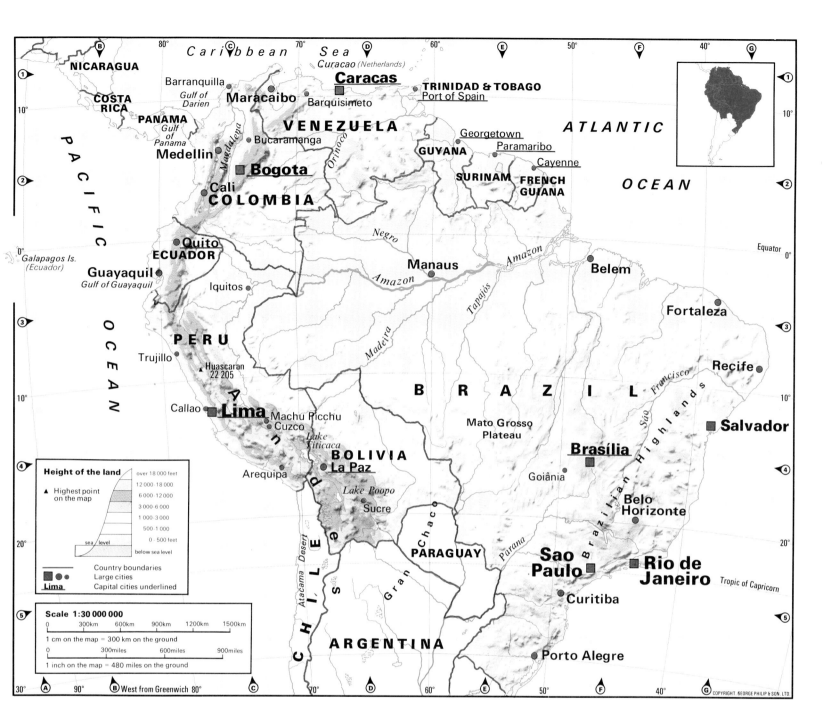

Height of the land

over 18 000 feet	
12 000 - 18 000	
6 000 - 12 000	
3 000 - 6 000	
1 000 - 3 000	
500 - 1 000	
0 - 500 feet	
below sea level	

▲ Highest point on the map

sea level

━━━ Country boundaries
■ ● ● Large cities
<u>Lima</u> Capital cities underlined

Scale 1:30 000 000

0   300km   600km   900km   1200km   1500km

1 cm on the map = 300 km on the ground

0   300miles   600miles   900miles

1 inch on the map = 480 miles on the ground

Cattle and cowboys. *To the south of the Amazon jungle, there is a large area of dry woodland and grassland in Brazil called the Mato Grosso. Cattle are grazed here, and horses are still used to round them up.*

Did you know?

Ecuador means *Equator*: the Equator (0°) crosses the country.

Colombia is named after Christopher *Columbus*, who sailed from Europe to the Americas in 1492.

Bolivia is named after Simon *Bolivar*, a hero of the country's war of independence in the 1820s.

La Paz, the biggest town in Bolivia, means *peace*. But there have been over 100 revolutions in Bolivia, the highest total in the world!

79

TEMPERATE SOUTH AMERICA

Chile is 2600 miles long, but only about 124 miles wide, because it is sandwiched between the Andes and the Pacific. In the *north* is the Atacama Desert, the driest in the world. In one place, there was no rain for 400 years! Fortunately, rivers from the Andes permit some irrigation. Chilean nitrates come from this area. Nitrates are salts in dried-up lakes; they are used to make fertilizers and explosives.

In the *center*, the climate is like the Mediterranean area and California, with hot dry summers and warm wet winters with westerly winds (six words begin with 'w': it's easy to remember!) This is a lovely climate, and most Chileans live in this area.

In the *south*, Chile is wet, windy and cool. Thick forests which include the Chilean pine (monkey puzzle tree) cover the steep hills. The reason for these contrasts is the wind. Winds bringing cloud and rain blow from the Pacific Ocean all year in the south; but only in winter in the center; and not at all in the north.

Geysers in the Andes, Chile. *Hot steam hisses into the cold air, 13,150 feet above sea level in the Andes of northern Chile.*

The Falkland Islands

These islands are a British colony in the South Atlantic. They are about 300 miles east of Argentina, which claims them as the Islas Malvinas. Britain fought an Argentine invasion in 1982, and the military force is now as large as the population (only 2000). Sheep farming is the main occupation.

The capital is Port Stanley and this is the only town. It has houses that look very much like English houses, but the remote farmhouses get their mail by 'mail drop' from a Beaver aircraft (see stamp above). Until recently, there were no roads to these farms. This stamp shows Argentina's claim that the Falkland Islands are part of Argentina.

The Andes

The Andes are over 4400 miles long, so they are the longest mountain range in the world. They are fold mountains, with a very steep western side, and a gentler eastern side. Most of the high peaks are volcanoes: they are the highest volcanoes in the world. Mount Aconcagua (22,835 feet) is an extinct volcano. Mount Guallatiri, in Chile, is the world's highest active volcano – it last erupted in 1969.

The higher you climb, the cooler it is. And the farther you travel from the Equator, the cooler it is. Therefore, the snowline in southern Chile is *much* lower than in northern Chile.

Argentina means 'silvery' in Spanish: some of the early settlers came to mine silver. But today, Argentina's most important product is cattle. Cool grasslands called the pampas are ideal for cattle grazing.

Argentina is a varied country: the northwest is hot and dry, and the south is cold and dry (see photograph). The frontier with Chile runs high along the top of the Andes.

Buenos Aires, the capital city, is the biggest city in South America; it has 10 million people. The name means 'good air', but gasoline fumes have now polluted the air.

Paraguay and **Uruguay** are two countries with small populations. Each country has under five million people. Nearly half the population of Uruguay lives in the capital city, Montevideo, which is on the coast. In contrast Paraguay is completely landlocked. Animal farming is the most important occupation in both these countries.

Sheep farming in Patagonia, Argentina. *Southern Argentina has a cool, dry climate. Very few people live there – but lots of sheep roam the extensive grasslands. There are almost as many sheep in Argentina as there are people.*

THE PACIFIC

This map shows half the world. Guess which place is farthest from a continent: it is somewhere in the South Pacific. The Pacific also includes the deepest place in the world: the Mariana Trench (36,161 feet deep). It would take over an hour for a steel ball weighing $1\frac{1}{4}$ pounds to fall to the bottom!

There are thousands of islands in the Pacific Ocean. Some are volcanic mountains, while many others are low, flat coral islands. Coral also grows round the volcanoes (see photograph below).

A few islands have valuable minerals – for example Nauru (phosphates) and Bougainville (copper). But most islanders are occupied in farming. Many tropical crops grow well; sugarcane, bananas and pineapple are important exports. Islands big enough for a full-sized airport, such as Fiji, the Samoas, Tahiti and Hawaii (see page 66), now get many globe-trotting tourists.

Moorea from the air. *The coral reef can be clearly seen around this island in French Polynesia; the reef makes it difficult for ships to reach the land.*

The island is steep and rugged: it is an old volcano. Notice the deep valleys dug by rivers. The white patches are clouds, not snow.

Easter Island, South Pacific. *These huge stone sculptures each weigh about 50 tons! They were cut long ago with simple stone axes, and lifted with ropes and ramps – an amazing achievement for people who had no metal, no wheels and no machines.*

Look for Easter Island on the map (in square U 11): it is one of the remotest places in the world. It is now owned by Chile, 2399 miles away in South America.

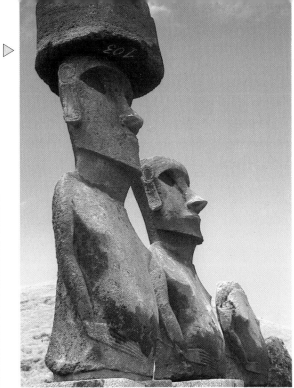

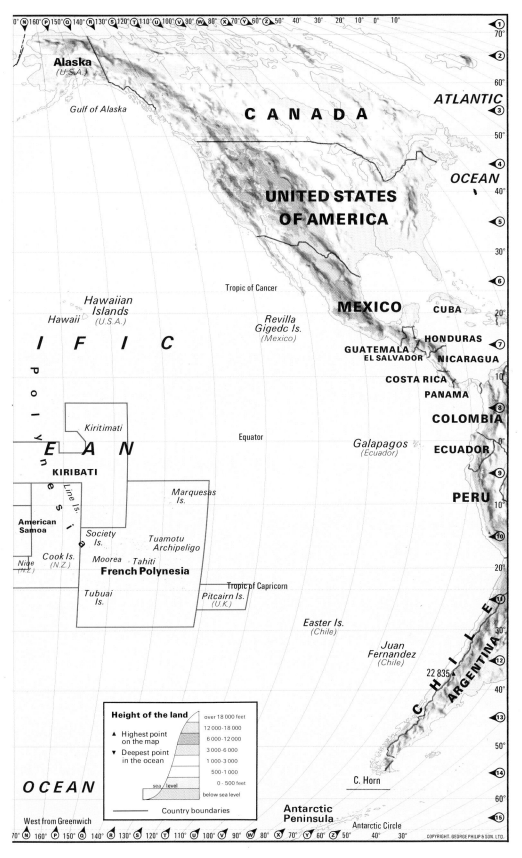

Most Pacific countries are large groups of small islands. Their boundaries are out at sea – just lines on a map. Kiribati is 33 small coral atolls spread over 1,930,000 square miles of ocean. And the Solomon Islands stretch for 900 miles. Imagine organizing something for the whole country!

Pacific stamps

The stamp from **French Polynesia** shows coconut palms – and an outrigger canoe: you can see how this makes the dugout canoe more stable at sea. In the background, there are canoes with sails.

In the highlands of **Papua New Guinea** (north of Australia), people live in round huts with thatched roofs. The stamp also shows the island's high, rugged mountains.

AUSTRALIA

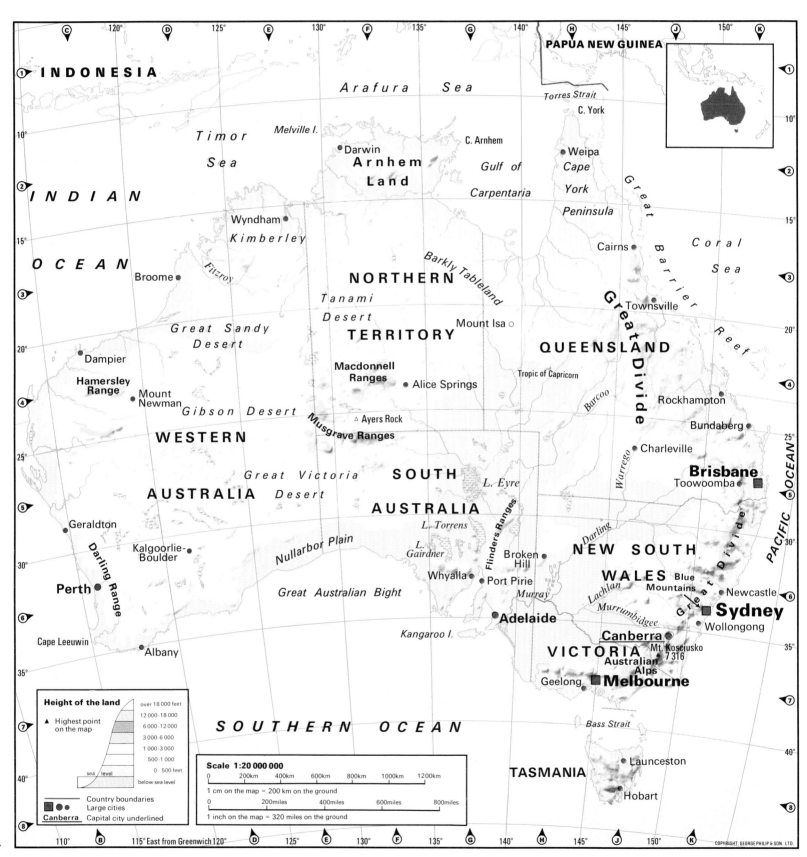

INDONESIA

Arafura Sea

Torres Strait

PAPUA NEW GUINEA

C. York

Timor

Melville I.

Darwin

C. Arnhem

Weipa

Cape

Sea

Arnhem
Land

Gulf of

York

INDIAN

Carpentaria

Peninsula

Wyndham

Great

Cairns

Coral

OCEAN

Kimberley

Fitzroy

Sea

Broome

NORTHERN

Barkly Tableland

Townsville

Tanami
Desert

Great Sandy
Desert

TERRITORY

Mount Isa ○

QUEENSLAND

Dampier

Macdonnell
Ranges

Alice Springs

Tropic of Capricorn

Hamersley
Range

Mount
Newman

Gibson Desert

Barcoo

Rockhampton

Bundaberg

△ Ayers Rock

Musgrave Ranges

WESTERN

Charleville

Great Victoria

SOUTH

Brisbane

AUSTRALIA

Desert

L. Eyre

Toowoomba

AUSTRALIA

Geraldton

L. Torrens

Darling

NEW SOUTH

Kalgoorlie-
Boulder

L.
Gairdner

Broken
Hill

WALES

Blue

Nullarbor Plain

Whyalla

Port Pirie

Lachlan

Mountains

Newcastle

Perth

Great Australian Bight

Murray

Murrumbidgee

Sydney

Adelaide

Wollongong

Cape Leeuwin

Kangaroo I.

Canberra

Albany

VICTORIA

Mt. Kosciusko
7316

Australian
Alps

Geelong

Melbourne

SOUTHERN   OCEAN

Bass Strait

Launceston

TASMANIA

Hobart

Height of the land

over 18 000 feet
12 000-18 000
6 000-12 000
3 000-6 000
1 000-3 000
500-1 000
0 - 500 feet
below sea level

▲ Highest point
on the map

sea level

Country boundaries

Large cities

Canberra   Capital city underlined

Scale 1:20 000 000

0   200km 400km 600km 800km 1000km 1200km

1 cm on the map = 200 km on the ground

0   200miles 400miles 600miles 800miles

1 inch on the map = 320 miles on the ground

84

115° East from Greenwich 120°

The Indian-Pacific Express

Town	Time	Day no.	Distance (miles)
Perth	9 p.m.	1	0
Kalgoorlie	7 a.m.	2	408
Port Pirie	2 p.m.	3	1515
Broken Hill	9 p.m.	3	1762
Sydney	4 p.m.	4	2461

It takes three nights and three days to cross Australia by train, from Perth to Sydney. The map shows you why the train is called the Indian-Pacific.

Australia is the world's largest island, but the smallest continent. It is the sixth-largest country in the world, smaller than the USA or Canada, but more than twice the size of India. Yet Australia has only about 16 million people. Most Australians are descended from people who came from Europe in the past 150 years.

The map shows that all the state capitals are on the coast, but Canberra, the national capital, is inland. Most Australians live in towns near the coast.

Only a few people live in the mountains or in the outback – the enormous area of semi-desert and desert that makes up most of the country. The few outback people live on huge sheep and cattle ranches, in mining towns, or on special reserves for the original Australians, the aborigines. Yet the wool, the meat and the minerals of the outback are important exports.

The Great Barrier Reef *is the world's largest living thing! It is an area of coral over 1240 miles long, which grows in the warm sea near the coast of Queensland.*

Ayers Rock *is in the heart of the desert in central Australia. Nothing grows on its steep sides. At sunset, it looks bright red!*

Christmas 'down under' *is in midsummer. Justine's stamp shows a typical Australian Christmas at the seaside, with swimming and sunbathing. But she didn't forget Santa Claus, with his red coat and his reindeer!*

Animals in Australia. *Australia is not joined to any other continent. It has been a separate island for millions of years, and has developed its own unique wildlife.*

The first stamps for the whole of Australia showed the country's most famous animal (far right). The kangaroo is a marsupial, which means 'pouched' – mother has her

own 'pocket' for baby Roo! Most of the world's marsupials live in Australia. Four of these animals are endangered species: they will die out unless they are protected.

NEW ZEALAND

The Antipodes

New Zealand is on the opposite side of the Earth from Europe. This double map shows that the far north of New Zealand is at the same latitude as North Africa, and that the far south of New Zealand is at the same latitude as Paris.

The New Zealand flag includes the British flag, because it was a British colony for over 100 years. Most New Zealand families originally came from Britain. The stars are known as the Southern Cross.

The three main islands that make up New Zealand are 1240 miles east of Australia. Only 3½ million people live in the whole country. The capital is Wellington, near the center of New Zealand, but the largest city is Auckland in the north.

The original inhabitants were the Maoris, but now they are only about 8 percent of the population. Some place-names are Maori words, such as Rotorua and Wanganui.

South Island is the largest island, but has fewer people than North Island. There are far more sheep than people! Mount Cook, the highest point in New Zealand (12,349 feet), is in the spectacular Southern Alps. Tourists visit the far south to see the glaciers and fjords. The fast-flowing rivers are used for hydroelectricity.

86

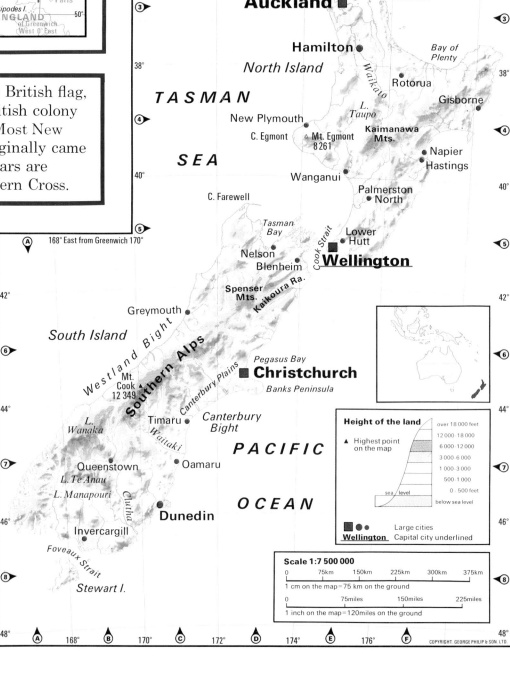

Height of the land

▲ Highest point on the map

over 18 000 feet
12 000-18 000
6 000-12 000
3 000-6 000
1 000-3 000
500-1 000
0 - 500 feet
below sea level

■ ● ● Large cities
Wellington Capital city underlined

Scale 1:7 500 000

0   75km   150km   225km   300km   375km
1 cm on the map = 75 km on the ground

0   75miles   150miles   225miles
1 inch on the map = 120 miles on the ground

COPYRIGHT GEORGE PHILIP & SON LTD.

A geothermal power station *in North Island. In this volcanic area there is natural hot steam underground which can be piped to power stations to produce electricity.*
▽

New Zealand Exports

These stamps show some major exports: pine trees become sawn timber for export (10c); sheep's wool is spun for export (18c); the 20-cent stamp shows cattle hides and skins being lifted onto a ship; while the 25-cent stamp shows cartons of New Zealand butter being loaded. Notice the snow-covered volcanic mountain in the background.

North Island has a warmer climate than South Island. In some places you can see hot springs and boiling mud pools and there are also volcanoes. Fine trees and giant ferns grow in the forests, but much of the forest has been cleared for farming. Cattle are kept on the rich grasslands for meat and milk. Many different kinds of fruit grow well, including apples and kiwi fruit.

Sheep grazing on the Canterbury Plains, *in South Island. New Zealand lamb is exported to Europe and North America in refrigerated ships. In the distance are the snow-covered Southern Alps. This great mountain range has glaciers, fjords and ski slopes.*
▽

ANTARCTIC

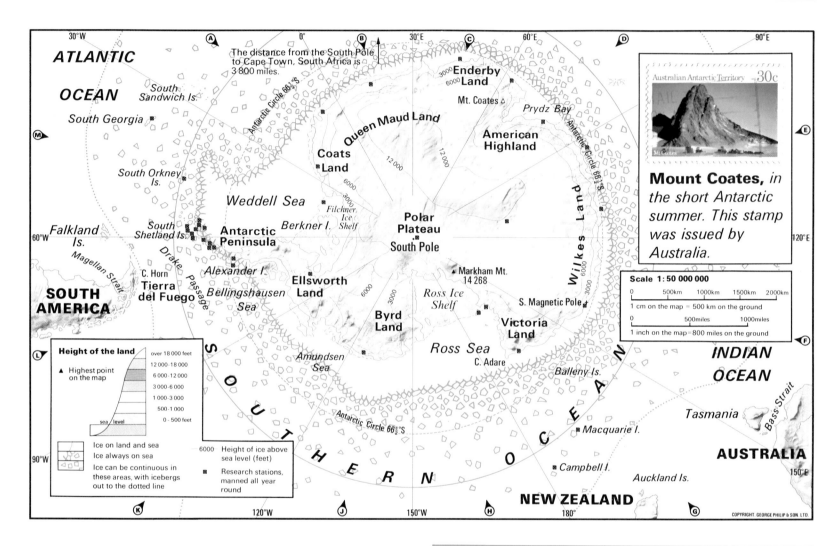

ATLANTIC

OCEAN

The distance from the South Pole to Cape Town, South Africa is 3 800 miles.

South Sandwich Is.

South Georgia

South Orkney Is.

Enderby Land

Mt. Coates

Prydz Bay

American Highland

Queen Maud Land

Coats Land

Weddell Sea

Filchner Ice Shelf

Berkner I.

Polar Plateau

South Pole

Wilkes Land

Falkland Is.

South Shetland Is.

Antarctic Peninsula

Magellan Strait

C. Horn

Tierra del Fuego

Alexander I.

Bellingshausen Sea

Ellsworth Land

Drake Passage

SOUTH AMERICA

Markham Mt. 14 268

Ross Ice Shelf

S. Magnetic Pole

Byrd Land

Victoria Land

Ross Sea

C. Adare

Amundsen Sea

Balleny Is.

INDIAN

OCEAN

Tasmania

Bass Strait

Macquarie I.

AUSTRALIA

Campbell I.

Auckland Is.

NEW ZEALAND

COPYRIGHT. GEORGE PHILIP & SON. LTD.

Australian Antarctic Territory 30c

Mt Coates

Mount Coates, *in the short Antarctic summer. This stamp was issued by Australia.*

Scale 1 : 50 000 000

0   500km   1000km   1500km   2000km

1 cm on the map = 500 km on the ground

0   500miles   1000miles

1 inch on the map = 800 miles on the ground

Height of the land

▲ Highest point on the map

over 18 000 feet
12 000-18 000
6 000-12 000
3 000-6 000
1 000-3 000
500-1 000
0 - 500 feet

sea level

Ice on land and sea
Ice always on sea
Ice can be continuous in these areas, with icebergs out to the dotted line

6000   Height of ice above sea level (feet)

▨   Research stations, manned all year round

Emperor penguins *with chicks. Penguins cannot fly, but they can swim very well. The parents use their feet to protect the eggs and chicks from the cold ice! No land animals live in Antarctica, but the ocean is full of fish, which provide food for penguins, seals and whales.*

▽

Fact box: Antarctica

5th largest continent – about 5,367,000 square miles

Surrounded by cold **seas**
South Pole **first reached** in 1911

Antarctica is the continent surrounding the South Pole. It is the coldest, windiest and iciest place in the world! It is also very isolated, as the map shows.

No people live in Antarctica permanently. Some scientists work in research stations.

Everything that is needed in Antarctica has to be brought in during the short summer. From November to January, icebreakers can reach the land. But huge icebergs are always a danger. In winter (May to July) it is always dark, the sea is frozen, and people have to face extreme cold and dangerous blizzards.

ARCTIC

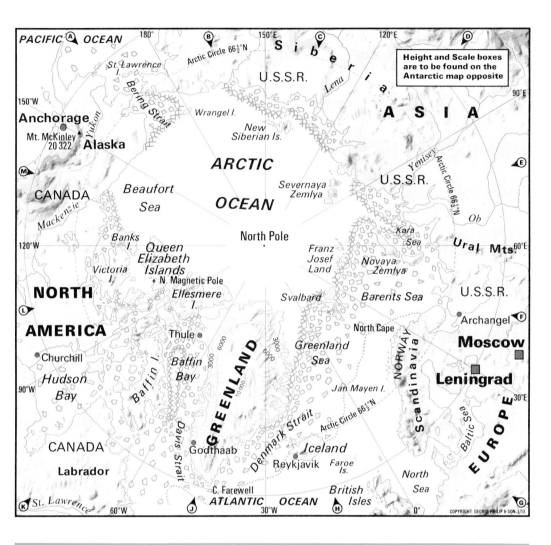

Height and Scale boxes are to be found on the Antarctic map opposite

COPYRIGHT. GEORGE PHILIP & SON, LTD.

The Arctic is an ocean, which is frozen throughout the winter. It is surrounded by the northernmost areas of three continents, but Greenland is the only truly Arctic country.

For most of the year the land is snow-covered. During the short summer, when the sun never sets, the snow and the frozen topsoil melt. But the deeper soil is still frozen, so the land is very marshy. This treeless landscape is called the tundra.

The reindeer and caribou can be herded or hunted, but farming is impossible. In recent years, rich mineral deposits have been found. Canada, the USA and USSR have military bases facing each other across the Arctic Ocean.

Eskimos. *The Inuit (Eskimos) have lived in the Arctic for thousands of years by hunting and fishing. These men* (left) *are resting their husky dogs which are trained to pull sledges.*

The Inuit only build igloos as emergency shelters. Most of them live in wooden buildings that are well insulated against the cold, like the Greenland family (above), *and most are more likely to travel by skimobile than by sledge. Many work in mining camps, military bases and weather stations.*

Fact box: Arctic

4th largest ocean – about 5,405,405 square miles

World record for least sunshine and tallest iceberg
Surrounded by cold **land**
North Pole **first reached** in 1909

QUIZ

Name the island

The name of the continent where each island is found is marked on each outline. Do you know (a) the name of each island and (b) to which country each island belongs (or are they island countries)?

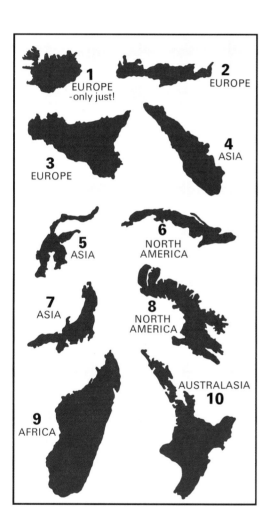

1 EUROPE -only just!

2 EUROPE

3 EUROPE

4 ASIA

5 ASIA

6 NORTH AMERICA

7 ASIA

8 NORTH AMERICA

9 AFRICA

10 AUSTRALASIA

Name the country

There is a long, thin country in almost every continent. Can you name the countries shown here – and name the continent in which they are found? (If you need help, look at pages 8–9 for a map of the countries of the world.)

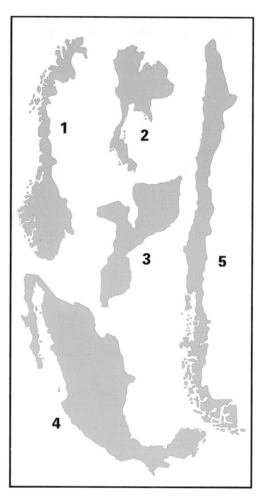

1

2

3

4

5

A mystery message

Use the map of the countries of the world on pages 8–9 to decode this message. Each missing word is all or part of the name of a country. (For some answers, letters have to be taken out of or added to the name of the country.)

I was ____a__ (east of Austria), so I bought a large _____ (east of Greece), some _____ns (east of Norway) and a bottle of ____ugal (west of Spain). Finally, I ate an ___land (west of Norway) -cream. I enjoyed my _e__l (east of Mauritania), but afterwards I began to ____earla (south of Romania) and I got a bad $____ (south of France). A ∅___ (east of Saudi Arabia) told me: 'Just eat Philip____sapples (south of Taiwan) and __gypt (east of Libya), cooked in a Ja___ (east of Korea). Tomorrow you can eat a Ghban___ (east of Ivory Coast) and some _____ (east of Peru) nuts. It shouldn't ____a Rica (west of Panama) you too much.' I said: 'You must be ___agascar (east of Mozambique)! I think I've got ____ysr__ (north of Indonesia). I'll have __/__ (west of Benin) to a doctor quickly, otherwise I'll soon be ____Sea (lake between Israel and Jordan).' Happily, the doctor __bared (island country south of USA) me, so I am still M__d___s (islands west of Sri Lanka) today!

Oceans and seas

What ocean would you cross on an airplane journey. . .
1 From Australia to the USA?
2 From Brazil to South Africa?
3 From Canada to the USSR?
4 From Madagascar to Indonesia?
5 From Mexico to Portugal?

What sea would you cross on an airplane journey. . .
6 From Saudi Arabia to Egypt?
7 From Korea to Japan?
8 From Denmark to the United Kingdom?
9 From Vietnam to the Philippines?
10 From Cuba to Colombia?

Places in Asia

Move the letters to find:

Countries
RAIN; CHAIN; MOAN; AWAIT N.
Capital cities
ANIMAL; I HELD; A BULK
KEG NIP; LOUSE; DIARY H.

Find the color

Each answer is a color. Use the atlas index and the maps to help you.

Cover the right-hand column with a piece of paper and try to answer the left-hand column only. Award yourself *2* points for each correct answer to the left-hand column only, or *1* point if you used the clues in both columns.

1 A sea between Egypt and Saudi Arabia. . .

2 A huge island east of Canada. . .

3 The sea between Turkey and the USSR. . .

4 The sea between Korea and China. . .

5 The sea on which Archangel lies, in the USSR. . .

6 A town in southern France which is also a fruit. . .

7 The tributary of the Nile River that flows from Ethiopia to Khartoum (Sudan). . .

. . .and the river on the border of Oklahoma and Texas.

. . .and a bay on the west side of Lake Michigan.

. . .and a forest in Germany.

. . .and a (stony?) river in Wyoming.

. . .and the river flowing north from Lake Victoria to Khartoum (Sudan).

. . .and the river which is the border between South Africa and Namibia.

. . .and a mountain ridge in eastern USA.

How well do you know the states of the USA?

All the answers can be found on the maps on pages 62–63 and 66–69. Do not include Alaska and Hawaii.

1 Which is the *biggest* state?
2 Which is the *smallest* state?
3 Which state reaches farthest *north*? (careful!)
4 Which state reaches farthest *south*?
5 Which state reaches farthest *west*?
6 Which state reaches farthest *east*?
7 Which state is split into two by a lake?
8 Which state is split into two by an inlet of the sea?
9 Which two states are perfect rectangles in shape?
10 Which state is shaped like a saucepan?
11 In which state would you be if you visited Lake Huron?
12 In which state would you be if you visited Lake Ontario?
13 In which state would you be if you visited the Great Salt Lake?
14 In which state would you be if you visited the Mississippi Delta?

15 Which state in *northern* USA is called South   ?
16 Which state in *southern* USA is called North   ?
17 There is only one place in the USA where four states meet: which states?
18 How many states have a border with Mexico?
19 How many states have a coastline on the Pacific?
20 How many states have a coastline on the Gulf of Mexico?

Great rivers of Europe

Use pages 18–39 to discover which great river flows through or near each pair of towns or cities.
1 Vienna, Austria and Budapest, Hungary.
2 Rotterdam, Netherlands and Bonn, Germany.
3 Avignon, France and Lyons, France.
4 Worcester, England and Gloucester, England.
5 Toledo, Spain and Lisbon, Portugal.

Things To Do

Where do the things you use come from?

What do you and your family use, eat or wear from different countries of the world? In this atlas you will find lists of some items we have found (pages 27 and 37). Now you can do some spotting.

Collect stamps with a theme

A stamp collection soon grows. Try a *thematic* collection: choose a theme (topic) and collect stamps on that theme. For example, you could collect: *Flags* on stamps. Togo had a flag stamp for Independence Day.

Map stamps: small islands often issue map stamps to show everyone where they are!

Traditional crafts on stamps: this Zambian thatcher is using a homemade ladder.

Make your own coin collection

Ask people who have been abroad for any foreign coins they do not want – you will have an instant collection! If you cannot have the coins to keep, you could make pencil or crayon rubbings on thin paper. Look at the pictures of coins in the atlas. Look at your coins for examples of languages; crops; famous buildings; historic events. . . .

INDEX

How to Use this Index

The first number given after each name or topic is the page number; then a letter and another number tell you which square of the map you should look at.

For example, Abidjan is in square B2 on page 56. Find B at the top or bottom of the map on page 56 and put a finger on it. Put another finger on the number 2 at the side of the map. Move your fingers in from the edge of the map and they will meet in square B2. Abidjan will now be easy to find. It is the capital city of the Ivory Coast, a country in West Africa.

If a name goes through more than one square, the square given in the index is the one in which the biggest part of the name falls.

Names like *Gulf of Mexico* and *Cape Horn* are in the Index as *Mexico, Gulf of* and *Horn, Cape*.

ANSWERS TO QUESTIONS

Answers to text questions

page 18 Western Europe's most important building: the Headquarters of the European Community in Brussels, the capital of Belgium. In this building many of the important decisions about Western Europe are made. The photograph shows reflections in the double-glazed windows. In the reflection you can see small old houses and shops and big modern office buildings in Brussels, the biggest city in Belgium.

page 19 B = Belgium; D = Germany (Deutschland in German); DK = Denmark; E = Spain (España); F = France; GB = Great Britain; GR = Greece; I = Italy; IRL = Ireland (Republic of Ireland); L = Luxembourg; NL = Netherlands; P = Portugal.

page 21 The London landmarks featured on the stamp are (*left to right*): Westminster Abbey; Nelson's column (in Trafalgar Square); statue of Eros in Piccadilly Circus; Telecom Tower; clock tower of the Houses of Parliament (containing the bell Big Ben); St Paul's Cathedral; Tower Bridge; White Tower of the Tower of London.

page 25 Belgium has two official languages, French and Flemish. The coin on the left has the French name for Belgium, that on the right its Flemish name.

page 27 The vegetables on the stall are green and red peppers, eggplant, onions and tomatoes, with some cucumbers and baby marrows on the left.

page 29 The international clock in Berlin: the names on the clock stay still; the numbers move

slowly round. In 24 hours, the numbers have turned a full circle – just like the Earth in space! When the photograph was taken, at 16.00 hours (4 p.m.) in Berlin, it was 13.30 hours (1.30 p.m.) in Reykjavik, Iceland, and 17.00 hours (5 p.m.) in Helsinki, Finland. In places *west* of Berlin it is earlier in the day; in places *east* of Berlin, it is later in the day. Note the names on the clock are in German.

page 55 Puzzle picture: the circles are 'drawn' by huge center pivot irrigation sprays, which turn slowly to make the shape of a circle. Each circle is about half a mile across. The irrigation allows crops to grow in the desert. Some of the crops in the circular 'fields' are already ripening, so they look less green.

page 57 Puzzle picture: this farmer in Ghana is making a mound of earth over each yam tuber he has planted.

page 62 The photograph of the fruit market shows (*at back*) bananas, pineapple; (*center*) breadfruit, mango, lime; (*at front*) grapefruit, lemons, papaya, pineapple. There are vegetables on display behind.

page 63 The north shores of Lakes Superior, Huron, Erie and Ontario are in Canada, and the south shores in the USA. Lake Michigan is entirely in the USA.

page 63 El Salvador only has a coastline on the Pacific Ocean. Belize only has a coastline on the Caribbean Sea. (Honduras has a tiny coastline on the Pacific – look closely at the map!)

page 67 Seattle to Miami is 3384

miles; New Orleans to Chicago is 925 miles.

page 69 The stamp shows the Mississippi River. It flows southward to New Orleans and the Gulf of Mexico. It was used for transport far into the heart of America long before roads were built, so it became known as the 'Great River Road'.

Answers to quiz

Name the island
(Name of country in parentheses after name of island)
1 Iceland (Iceland); 2 Crete (Greece); 3 Sicily (Italy); 4 Sumatra (Indonesia); 5 Sulawesi (Indonesia); 6 Cuba (Cuba); 7 Honshu (Japan); 8 Baffin Island (Canada); 9 Madagascar (Madagascar); 10 North Island (New Zealand).

Name the country
(Name of continent in parentheses after name of country)
1 Norway (Europe); 2 Thailand (Asia); 3 Mozambique (Africa); 4 Mexico (Central America); 5 Chile (South America).

Oceans and seas
1 Pacific; 2 Atlantic; 3 Arctic; 4 Indian; 5 Atlantic; 6 Red Sea; 7 Sea of Japan; 8 North Sea; 9 South China Sea; 10 Caribbean Sea.

A mystery message
I was *hungry*, so I bought a large *turkey*, some *swedes* and a bottle of *port*. Finally, I ate an *ice*-cream. I enjoyed my *meal*, but afterwards I began to *bulge* and I got a bad *pain*. A *man* told me: 'Just eat *pineapple*s and *egg* cooked in a *pan*. Tomorrow you can eat a *banana* and some *Brazil* nuts. It

shouldn't *cost* you too much.' I said: 'You must be *mad*! I think I've got *malaria*. I'll have *to go* to a doctor quickly, otherwise I'll soon be *dead*.'
  Happily, the doctor *cured* me, so I am still *alive* today!

Places in Asia
Countries Iran; China; Oman; Taiwan.
Capital cities Manila; Delhi; Kabul; Peking; Seoul; Riyadh.

Color quiz
1 Red (Red Sea/Red River);
2 Green (Greenland/Green Bay);
3 Black (Black Sea/Black Forest);
4 Yellow (Yellow Sea/Yellowstone River); 5 White (White Sea/White Nile); 6 Orange (Orange/Orange River); 7 Blue (Blue Nile/Blue Ridge, USA).

Score
13–14 Brilliant! 10–12 Very well done. 6–9 Good. 2–5 Use this atlas more – you'll soon do better. 0–1 Try another planet – there's less geography there.

States of the USA
1 Texas; 2 Rhode Island; 3 Minnesota; 4 Florida; 5 California; 6 Maine; 7 Michigan; 8 Maryland; 9 Wyoming and Colorado; 10 Oklahoma; 11 Michigan; 12 New York; 13 Utah; 14 Louisiana; 15 South Dakota; 16 North Carolina; 17 Utah, Colorado, Arizona and New Mexico; 18 Four; 19 Three; 20 Five.

Great rivers of Europe
1 Danube; 2 Rhine; 3 Rhône; 4 Severn; 5 Tagus.

Illustration Acknowledgements
The Australian Tourist Commission p. 85 (top); *Bruce Coleman Limited* p. 6, p. 8, p. 11 (right), p. 15 (left), p. 21 (below right), p. 23 (above right), p. 27 (top), p. 29 (below left), p. 32 (below), p. 37 (top), p. 39 (below), p. 40, p. 54 (top), p. 59, p. 61 (right), p. 69 (above left), p. 70 (top left and below), p. 72 (top), p. 78 (top), p. 80 (below), p. 82, p. 83, p. 87, p. 89

(below); *The Daily Telegraph* p. 5; *Susan Griggs* p. 11 (left), p. 21 (top), p. 23 (below right), p. 31 (top), p. 33, p. 38, p. 39 (top), p. 42 (right), p. 43 (top), p. 45 (below), p. 50 (above left), p. 62, p. 63, p. 65 (right), p. 67, p. 70 (top right), p. 72 (below), p. 73, p. 76; *Robert Harding Picture Library* p. 15 (right), p. 19, p. 41, p. 45 (center), p. 47 (top), p. 49 (center and below left),

p. 50 (below), p. 58 (below left), p. 61 (left), p. 64 (left), p. 75 (top left), p. 78 (below left), p. 88; *The J. Allan Cash Photolibrary* p. 12, p. 25 (below right), p. 29 (top), p. 31 (below left), p. 45 (top), p. 48, p. 50 (above right), p. 54 (below left), p. 56, p. 57 (top left), p. 58 (top and below left), p. 75 (below), p. 78 (below right); *NASA* title page, p. 55 (below left); *The Quentin Bell*

Organisation p. 64 (right); *Ralph Somerville* p. 49 (top); *Spanish National Tourist Office* p. 31 (center); *Vautier-de-Nanxe* p. 42 (left), p. 71, p. 77, p. 80 (top), p. 81; *David and Jill Wright* p. 10, p. 14, p. 16, p. 18, p. 21 (below right), p. 22, p. 23 (below left), p. 25 (top and below left), p. 27 (center and below), p. 29 (top), p. 31 (below right), p. 34 (left), p. 35, p.43

(below), p. 44, p. 47 (below left), p. 52, p. 54 (below right), p. 57 (top right, center and below), p. 60, p. 68 (above), p. 69 (center and top right), p. 75 (top right), p. 85 (center); *Zefa* p. 11 (center), p. 20, p. 23 (above left), p. 24, p. 28, p. 32 (top), p. 34 (right), p. 37 (below, right and left), p. 53, p. 55 (below right), p. 65 (left), p. 68 (below), p. 79, p. 89 (center).